Life Happens:
Bounce Back!

Tasfil Publishing LLC

New Jersey, USA
www.tasfil.com

Copyright © 2015 Lisa Bien

All rights reserved, including the right of reproduction in whole or in part in any form.

Cover Design: Laura Jacoby

Back Cover Photography: Dana Romano Photography

ISBN: 09862580-1-6

ISBN-13: 978-0986258015

Other books by this author:

Divorce Happens: Bounce Back!

Dedication

This book is dedicated to my sons,
Jacob and Ari.

You are my heart, light, and the greatest gift
I have ever received.

It's an honor and a privilege to be your mom.

I hope as you go through life, you will always
bounce back—with laughter and love.

Why I Wrote This Book

I wrote this book for you. I want to share a story with you to let you know you are not alone during the inevitable low points and struggles in your life.

I wrote this book for my dear friend's daughter who is beautiful and smart, yet insecure and sad. I want to help her change her outlook, make her smile, and show her how to love who she is. When she learns to do that, she will find the inner strength to overcome any obstacles life throws at her.

Ultimately, I wrote this book to remind every one of us that we are all responsible for our own happiness. Every day when you wake up, you have a choice on how you want to approach the day, and hence the rest of your life. *You* get to decide. Life is an abundance of choices, but the first choice is to decide how you are going to live today. Right now.

We all struggle with and through bad self-esteem and negative self-images. Sometimes we don't even realize it until life hits us in the ass with a major problem or potential catastrophe. It is my goal to help you see how beautiful you truly are and to inspire you to love yourself. When can recognize your beauty and value the incredible being that you are, you will be better able to bounce back from the low points in your life. And hopefully, you will never such a low point, or at least have fewer, because you will have learned to make choices from the perspective of a healthy self-esteem and positive self-image.

I want everybody to know that we can change, if we truly desire to do so.

Table of Contents

Life Happens: Bounce Back!

Foreword

Your journey has begun. By opening the pages of this book, you have embarked on a process that will be emotional, enlightening, challenging, and, in the end, the most profound change of your life.

In all my years of working so closely with a broad range of people and being trusted in the most intimate way, I have come to understand a universal truth: Each and every one of us harbors a deep and painful aspect of who we are. No matter how charmed one's life may seem, underneath there lies a unique pain. Each of us walks around in our own special way trying to cope with pain that can cast a shadow over us. The origin of our pain has no limits, no boundaries, and could be formed from any number of factors in our life, such as dynamics in our family, the slight of a friend in school, or the heartbreak of our first love. The list is endless.

Equally powerful and most important is how each of us manages the pain that has come to be a driving factor in our life. Like it or not, most challenges we encounter are directly tied to our coping rather than the pain itself. Many a time a person has entered my office in the hopes of resolving a particular pain or hurt. Clearly, my compassion is immediately expressed, while in my head I evaluate the ways this person has coped with their pain, and the path this coping has sent them on. The journey of true and sustaining growth and change arises from addressing both the pain itself and the patterns we have developed to cope with the pain.

No one can deny that foraying into the heart of this journey of change can be daunting and intimidating. Therefore, one of the most significant catalysts to a successful change and the ability to bounce back entails a guide who can educate, support, encourage, and essentially serve as your champion, reminding you that you are worth all the effort and reward this journey of bouncing back will bring.

As you venture into the heart of this book, you will find yourself in the hands of one of the most seasoned guides you could envision. Lisa Bien is a woman who has found herself in the depths of life's pain. Her pain and subsequent coping mechanisms led her down a path from which she has bounced back.

The following pages are her personal account of the journey that she herself lived and breathed. The wisdom she offers is no off-the-shelf or cookie-cutter variety. She leads you through her own experiences. Who better to hold your hand along this journey than a woman who has ventured out of the pain and launched herself to a level of contentment and joy that she never foresaw for herself until not that many years ago?

When I first encountered Lisa, I found myself in the presence of a tremendously gifted woman who was encased in some profoundly destructive coping mechanisms. You could see her heart and feel the gifts of humor, relationship building, parenting, and genuine passion for life. Unfortunately, the tools she relied upon for coping shackled her to a continuous pattern of self-destruction. As much as she desired change in her life, she repeatedly found herself at the starting line once again.

As this book reveals, she systematically and courageously took one step at a time to bounce back from earlier pains in her life and the destructive behaviors that resulted. The woman I know now is all that she was meant to be. Lisa has bounced back. She is now your guide on your own journey of bouncing back.

Many a self-help book has been written, and many more are to come. The one you hold in your hands, however, is special. I strongly encourage you to heed the words that are to follow because each and every insight Lisa shares has come from her own experiences. She knows, because she has been there.

Dr. Michael Plumeri
Clinical Psychologist

During my short twenty-four years, the women I have carefully watched, even imitated, tend to linger and hesitate when it comes to making the decisions in their lives that could change everything--the leaps of faith that could threaten their very senses of security or comfort with one resounding, open-ended yet ever terrifying question: "What if?"

What I love about Lisa and her commitment to bouncing back is her staunch determination to never just ask the question but to discover every possible answer. When I first met the one and only Bien, I was standing on that exact precipice, asking "What if?" but not daring to take a step further. Lisa was brazenly, painfully honest when she asked me what I was afraid of, and she struck a perfect balance with her unconditional support and demand for "better" when all my answers fell short.

We so seldom step back from the canvas of our lives to observe, feel, evaluate, and assess what we have thus far created for our lives. We are so afraid to erase the parts we have come to dislike, resent, and suffer through, for fear of rocking the boat and failure. But when a woman like Lisa Bien writes a book like this, and puts your own brush back into your own hand once and for all, it is irresistible to not only ask, "What if?" but to start imagining, sketching, and creating the life you want, all over again.

She teaches us that self-love is the landscape that our lives and the best versions of ourselves are built on. When she encourages us to bounce back, she reminds us that our lives are always and continually ours to claim—at any age, at any phase, and with all our unique and vibrant colors.

Thank you, Lisa, for pioneering this message. May it always serve as a testament to the human will and the very best life still to come.

Anna Tate
Former Student and Mentee

I have always known Lisa to be positive and encouraging, motivating and honest, and more than anything, genuine in her desire for others to succeed.

Lisa was candid about her moments of weakness. She didn't hide her low points. She was never too proud to be defeated, but she was too strong to let a failed relationship, a lost job, or broken friendships overcome her. As a young woman, I admired the braveness and candor of an active and successful married mother of two who seemed to be living a perfect life. She had the husband, the job, handsome and well-mannered sons, and a full social life. But unknown to many, she was unhappy.

Knowing yourself and being honest with yourself is a feat, and a scary one at that. Lisa not only faced defeat, she embraced it, learned from it, and grew from it.

She has always been a valued mentor and friend of mine. It's an easy, low-maintenance friendship, unlike so many friendships among women today. Very recently, I had my own moment of failure. Turning to her for insight offered instant clarity. There was no quick fix for my problem.

As Lisa said, "What's done is done," but she helped me see that it wasn't the earth-shattering, world-ending issue that I was making it out to be. By speaking to her, I came to terms with how low I was feeling, and moved on. We had a plan of action in place, and what had felt like such a negative, quickly became a win-win. In the grand scheme of things, my problem was minor. But by owning it, and facing it with Lisa's help, I was able to bounce back. And you will, too.

On Lisa's way back up from her low points, she often spoke of "getting healthy," not in the sense that she was mentally ill or unstable, but meaning that she was gaining clarity, seeing and understanding herself and her relationships better than ever. There was much introspection and self-evaluation. She had a path and a process, and it was working little by little every day. It took time, but she "got healthy" and never, ever looked back.

Kathleen Toy
Former Colleague and Mentee

I've known Lisa from the very beginning of her career, and I was lucky to work with her twice. We even became business partners! Through it all, there was one aspect of our work that actually wasn't "work" that she loved. It was mentoring others. It was truly her joy. Students would come to visit her, and she would spend time helping them with their resumes and providing guidance about their futures. They would leave, and she would always say the same thing, "I LOVE doing this! I wish I could always help other people, especially young people as they embark on their careers."

Lisa, look at you now! You are doing so much mentoring. Through teaching, your television program, and your book, you are making an impact on thousands. I am so proud of you for making your own dreams come true. I am equally proud of you for doing it all so well. Congratulations!

Sharla Feldscher
President, Sharla Feldscher Public Relations

Lisa Bien is a natural-born teacher, mentor, and friend. It came as no surprise to me that she decided to share her story of "bouncing back" to help others who could benefit from her triumphs and tribulations.

In 1996, she gave me my first job in public relations where we worked side by side for an elite agency in Philadelphia. It was there that I first witnessed her capacity for kindness, strength, and friendship. Her ability to foster friendships over the years has always boggled my mind. Despite kids, husbands, and careers, she manages to keep healthy, rewarding friendships.

A woman with endless energy, Lisa is a fighter. Her battles are of the heart, and her loyalty and pride are her ammunition. In the end, as she notes in her book, she learned that it is within yourself that you find happiness, contentment, and the glory of winning.

Garden Wellington-Logan
Public Relations Professional
and Lucky Friend of Big Red

Introduction

Here's my recommendation: do not buy this book, or any other self-help book for that matter, if you are unhappy and want to feel better, but you do not want to do the work.

Being happy and getting to a place of self-awareness and self-love takes a lot of hard work. Believe me, I know! Every day I continue to struggle and deal with issues from my childhood. But it's so worth the effort. I promise you: if you work hard, you will create a better life for yourself. You just have to be willing to commit to it and do the work.

What do I mean by doing the work? I mean taking stock of your behaviors and your patterns. Examining them closely and determining which are preventing you from living the happy life you want to live. And then you have to ask yourself if you are you willing to change those behaviors and patterns.

If the answer is *yes*, the next step is to find a way to create the changes you want so you can bounce back from your place of unhappiness. With this book, I'm providing you a way to do just that. I call it my *Four-step Bounce Back Into You* plan. I not only created it, I followed it. And I continue to live it. I know it works. But I also know it can be a hard plan to follow. Why?

Think about this: how many times do we hear people say, "I just want to lose twenty pounds," and they never do? Yet they know what to do to lose weight. We all do. Eat less, work out, and then you will get the results you want, right? But how many of us are really willing to do the work to create that change?

Self-help books are like diets and exercise: you only find success if you do the work. That's something else that I know to be true from my personal experience. I can't tell you how many times throughout my life that I went into a bookstore and wound up in the self-help section. I'd spend a lot of money and take the books home. Yes, I would feel better after I read them. I would even practice some of the exercises. However, in the end, I'd revert to me and my feelings of low self-esteem, of not feeling good enough, and being unhappy because I wasn't willing to do the work to create the change. I don't want my book to be that way for you.

In fact, I hope my book helps you want to do the work. What I discovered on my own was that I had to find myself worthy of doing the work in order to make that change happen. I had to learn to love myself enough to feel deserving of the work.

It wasn't easy and it wasn't quick. It took me several years to become the happy and contented person I am today. Prior to that, I'd spent too much time being scared and alone, all the while wanting to be happy and to have healthy relationships. I could make a list of relationships that simply were not working for me. But I knew before I could fix any of them, I needed to take a look at the one common denominator in all of them: me. So I decided to take a look at myself, at my patterns, my behaviors, and at no one else. My book will show you how to do the same thing to create the change you want to create and hopefully, since I'm giving you a plan, it won't take you as long as it took me!

My book is here to say: this is my story. In fact, you'll get a mini-autobiography of my life in the first couple of chapters. I wrote that so you will know exactly where I'm coming from, exactly how I ended up where I did, and exactly how I was able to change. Like I said, I know firsthand how incredibly hard and scary it is to change. I also know how important it is to do so if you want to break free of the negative patterns that are preventing you from being happy. And I am presenting to you, in this book, the method I found that works for me.

As I write this introduction now, I am the happiest I have ever been. Why? Because even though life is hard, with good days and bad days, I finally love me! I love the person I am and what I stand for. I am in no way perfect, but I can truly say, I love me, myself, and I!

Because I love myself, I continue to work hard at being happy. It's a choice I make every day. I always have two people in my head. The first is the little-girl Lisa who often talks to me, telling me negative things from my past that I grew up and spent the first part of my adult life repeating over and over. The second is the adult, Now Lisa, who fights those messages, feels alive, and loves her life. Both make me who I am today, but make no mistake about it, the messages we develop as a child never go away. They are always with us. It's up to us to learn how to understand the messages and not allow the past to negatively influence the future.

I did not write this book to simply share my life. I wrote it to remind you that if you do not have the life you want, if you want to change your life, create something new and wonderful, you can do it. I am proof.

I always knew I wanted to make a difference. I didn't know how or when, but now I do. It's by sharing my story with you. I'm letting you know that there is no one answer or secret about how to be happy and live the life of your dreams, except to take the time to fall in love with yourself and become the best version of YOU.

As you read the opening chapters, you'll notice a common theme running throughout my life: I have had no choice but to bounce back, to try to find the humor and opportunity in my story, laugh as much as possible, and to remember to love and believe in myself. That approach has worked and continues to work for me to get through this thing called life. As I take you through my story, I will share ideas and tips that helped me grow personally and professionally.

When my dear friend Laura says to me, "I'm sorry, sweetheart, that this happened," I always respond with: "You know me, I always bounce back." And now, I bounce with a big smile on my face because I have finally found the love I was always looking for: self-love.

Believe in yourself
and the rest of your
life will fall
into place.

As I just explained in the introduction, in the first section of the book I tell you a little about my life. I talk about both my childhood and adulthood to show you where I'm coming from. I discuss how I developed negative beliefs about myself, how those beliefs manifested negative life experiences that, in turn, encouraged me to develop more negative beliefs about myself. I show you how the cycle continued until I learned to stop the beliefs, which allowed me to start creating the life I always wanted.

In the second section, I detail my *Four-step Bounce Back Into You* plan. That plan is what I used to stop the negative cycle. I have personally done every step, so I can promise you it works. The first three steps take twenty-one days each and are followed by an evaluation week. Step Four is a brief period of reflection and evaluation of the whole plan so you can get started on the upward momentum of your own bounce back journey.

In short, the plan looks like this:

- Step 1: Get Clarity. Recognize the situations in your life that are making you unhappy and the underlying beliefs that helped create those situations.
- Step 2: Get Real. Determine exactly what your responsibilities and roles are in your negative situations.
- Step 3: Get a Vision. Figure out what the best version of you is and what kind of life you really want to have.
- Step 4: Get Going! Create a plan to change your beliefs so that you can create the life you want.

As you read through the steps, you will discover I repeatedly put emphasis on how important it is that we all learn to love ourselves. That's because the biggest lesson I've learned in my life is that I cannot recover from adversity and I cannot heal from being harmed—that is, I cannot bounce back when life happens—if I don't love and appreciate myself unconditionally.

Because I believe achieving self-love is the only way to ever achieve real happiness, the third section of the book is dedicated to providing a variety of exercises and practices to help you have the greatest love affair of your life: with yourself!

By working to love yourself and maintaining that love, no matter what happens in your life, you will always have the personal strength and ability to Bounce Back.

Section 1
My Story

Chapter One:
Growing up in Northeast Philadelphia

I am so proud of the fact that I grew up in a blue-collar neighborhood in northeast Philadelphia. It's an area where everyone worked hard, had a strong work ethic, and cared about each other. I love Philadelphia. It will always be one of my favorite cities.

We lived on a great street with lots of kids; the kids, for the most part, were all friends and we were always outside playing. It was a very simple childhood, nothing exciting. Both of my parents worked. My dad, a gutsy, good-hearted man who is legally considered my stepfather, loved us, raised us with my mother, and worked two jobs to support us. Throughout the book, I will refer to him as Dad.

My parents were divorced when I was two years old. No one ever talked to me about my biological father. All I knew was he and Mom got divorced. I never really saw much of him after that.

I have two older brothers to whom I was very close as a child. I am the youngest and I always looked up to my brothers. In my young eyes, my brothers could do no wrong.

I had one grandfather and three grandmothers. They were my favorite part of my childhood. I always felt special because I had three of the world's best grandmothers in my life. Each one was special. My favorite was my mother's mom, Mom-Mom. She had red hair, green eyes, and always had a wonderful smile for me. To this day, every time I watch the *I Love Lucy Show* or *That Girl*, I remember Mom-Mom fondly because I enjoyed spending time with her watching those shows. I loved being with all of my grandmothers, and I will always honor the wonderful memories of each of them.

I was blessed to have some truly great women in my life at a very early age, including my aunt. She has always been like a second mother to me, and she is someone I can count on for anything. Through the years, my aunt has taught me how to love unconditionally.

We had a nice life and, compared to some people, I would say it was a nice childhood. We just didn't communicate. If we were angry with one another or had something to say, we didn't say it. If my dad got upset with us, he stopped speaking to us, sometimes for weeks. This is where I learned not to disagree with anyone out of the fear that that person would stop talking to me. Or, conversely, I would stop talking to someone who upset me.

I now understand that the unhealthy habits of your parents can impact you as a child and that those habits, if left unchanged, will also impact you in your adult life. But I also understand that it's fixable. Yes, we are born preconditioned to some things but we are unconsciously taught other things, and those other things are the things we can change.

I think, in part, the problem my family had with communicating is what encouraged me, at a very young age, to start feeling like I wasn't good enough. It stemmed from my parents getting a divorce and my biological father not wanting to be in my life. He left us because he was not capable of being a dad to us while starting a second family. So he chose to be with his new wife and her kids. That decision impacted me for years. All I ever wanted to know was, why? *Why did you leave me? Why didn't you want me? Why didn't you want to know me?* Because no one would talk about his decisions and explain to me that his actions had nothing to do with me, I did what many children do: I blamed myself for his absence.

His decision made me feel "less-than," abandoned, and not good enough. I wanted my biological father to love me enough to fight for me to be in his life. But he didn't. And in my very young mind, I decided it was because I wasn't worthy enough for him. Maybe I wasn't worthy enough for love.

And so my story began.

The impact of the divorce went beyond just me and my feeling unworthy of my father's love. I remember always feeling different because of it, as if I was the only girl in the world whose parents were divorced. Remember, this was in the seventies and divorce wasn't as prevalent back then as it is now. I stood out because of the divorce. One day when I was having lunch at school, this girl turned to me and asked what it was like to have parents who were divorced. I remember believing she, and probably a lot of the other kids, thought I was odd and unusual.

Not only was I the odd girl with divorced parents, but I was one of the few Jewish girls, too. While all the kids in the neighborhood were usually nice to us, most of them were Catholic. Our family had different holidays. Our family went to a synagogue, not a church. And we went on Saturdays, not Sundays. Most of the kids didn't understand why we were different. Some of them were mean and called me names. So I became the odd girl with divorced parents and a weird religion.

If that wasn't enough, I was also the tall girl in the class. And picture this: in the seventies, I had curly, thick hair when every girl wanted Farrah Fawcett hair. I, too, wanted her sexy hair. But my hairstylist had Dorothy Hamill on the brain and *poof!* My thick and coarse hair formed this lovely brown bird's nest on top of my head, prompting the nickname Bird's Nest Bien. Imagine you're tall, and now you have a nest on your head. Attractive, huh?

And there you have it. A tiny, relatively insignificant event we have all suffered (a bad haircut) instilled deep feelings of not being all that pretty. Suddenly, I wasn't just odd, tall and different, I was unattractive, too.

When junior high rolled around, I discovered the cool crowd and thought if I could become cool, all my problems would be solved. Being cool became my goal. I believed if I were cool, then everyone would like me. It was so important to me to be liked, because if I was liked, then I was accepted, and if I was accepted, then that meant I was good enough, right? So it only made sense to me that I should start smoking cigarettes. That's what the cool kids did and I would look cool if I did it, too.

Smoking didn't work. I just couldn't get cool enough to feel accepted. So I amped things up in high school. I started experimenting with drugs.

I flunked ninth grade because I was too busy doing drugs and trying to act like I was "too cool for school." My mom, who throughout my life was always my advocate, insisted I attend summer school. She was tough on me. She loved me enough to pull me away from the kids I was hanging out with and to say "enough." It was the worst summer of my life. I didn't want to do summer school ever again. I felt so inadequate, less than. I was more of a loser in my head than ever before because, after all, who flunks out of ninth grade?

I had believed that taking drugs would help me fit into a group, but I was so wrong. The only lesson I learned about taking drugs was I ended up worse off than when I started. And I still was not in the cool crowd that I so desired to be in. Instead, I was in the "you-are-going-to-summer school" crowd. Drugs didn't help me get into the right crowd; drugs were not the answer and never are.

After junior high, many of the Jewish kids in my neighborhood decided to transfer high schools in the tenth grade so that they could attend a school with a greater population of Jewish kids. As a kid, I was not comfortable with my Judaism. As I mentioned, the predominant people in my neighborhood were not Jewish. Many of the kids made fun of me. So you would think that by going to a Jewish high school, I'd feel like I was finally finding a place where I belonged, where I wouldn't be different.

But that's not what happened.

Transferring to a new high school in tenth grade basically meant I had to start all over socially. The new school was in a highly populated Jewish area in northeast Philly. So, on top of not feeling good enough for my biological father to stick around and feeling like an unattractive flunky, I had a new group to compare myself to and come up lacking. I was in the midst of Jewish American Princess central. All those girls were prettier, smarter, thinner, and richer than I was. You name it, they had it all over me. Well, at least that's what I believed at the time.

Although I never believed in myself, I found someone in high school who did: my best friend, Sharyn. Somehow she saw something in me I didn't see. In fact, she seemed to believe in me more than I did. Sharyn was, and continues to be, one of my biggest cheerleaders. We had gym class together in tenth grade. She was athletic, and I was not. We had to jump over "the horse," that ancient piece of gym equipment that old-school gym teachers thought all kids should be able to jump over. To me, it was a big jump. I would run up, get close, and then stop. I was afraid I would fall when I jumped over.

Sharyn realized I was afraid to fall. She stood up in front of the entire class and said, "Come on, Lisa, you can do this! I will not let you fall. I will stand here and catch you." I ran up to the horse, jumped over, and she grabbed me so I did not fall. It felt great! I made it over.

Even with Sharyn by my side, I pretty much hated high school because I never felt that I fit in. I would bounce from one group to the next, never feeling a connection to any of them. And they didn't seem to want to connect to me. I was not the pretty girl. I was not the popular girl. I was a misfit. Being a misfit in high school was not fun.

All I wanted was to fit in and have a group of friends that I could call my own. And I did eventually discover some really cool people who at the time were just like me: they didn't fit into one particular group, either. Unintentionally, we formed our own. Today, I would say it was an eclectic group of friends. Others might still call us misfits, but whatever the name, along with Sharyn, those kids got me through high school.

I had been so focused on trying to fit in and be part of a group throughout high school that I never considered what would happen to me after high school. Right before graduation, I remember saying to my mom, "Wow, now that I am graduating from high school, I can do anything I want." Unfortunately, I had no idea what that was. I had no direction. So I decided to apply to college with a friend from school. How cool would that be? We would go to the same school and be college roommates. Well, that lasted for one semester because my friend hated the school and left. Suddenly, I was alone in college with no idea what to study and trying to make friends and find my way as a freshman.

My college years were not my best years. The behaviors I practiced in high school, I perfected in college. I finally found a way to be the cool girl.

I started drinking on a regular basis. Basically, every night at college is an excuse, a reason, and an opportunity to drink, if you want to. Of course, smoking was part of drinking. I became the party girl, and in my mind, the party kids were the fun, cool kids to hang out with. Remember, I always wanted to be in with the cool kids, so I could feel accepted and valued, and then that would mean I was good enough. I found that being the funny girl and the party girl made me the girl people wanted to hang out with. They nicknamed me "Joan" for Joan Rivers, because people said I sounded like her and was funny like her.

Unfortunately, the partying that was required to be Joan, didn't leave much time for studying. My GPA almost became a negative number and my self-image took another hit because of my grades.

I blamed my poor academic performance on the fact that I didn't have a direction in my life. At that time, I didn't know enough to stop the behaviors that were not working for me—the drinking, the partying, the constant worry about what other people thought of me and whether I fit in with them. But I did know enough to realize I was lost.

I saw other people behaving differently in ways that proved positive for them. My friends were continuing with their education, getting jobs, and buying cars. I didn't have a path or a vision. I didn't know who I was.

So after my first year in college, I decided I should take some time off to decide what I wanted to do with my life. It was the first time I told myself to stop, think, and then proceed. I remember literally asking myself: "What am I going to do with my life?"

Up to that point, all I knew how to do was to work hard and make money. It was something I'd learned from my parents. They had instilled a strong work ethic in my brothers and me. I had always worked, whether I waitressed or worked in retail. I was never afraid of hard work. And I began to realize that maybe I should apply that work ethic to myself and see what I could make with my life.

Taking time off from the treadmill of my life worked. It helped me get clarity and create a vision for my future. I guess you could say it was the first time I made an effort to bounce back from a very bad place. Unfortunately, I didn't have all the tools to do the job right, yet.

Looking back, I can see how my early years framed me for the young adult I became. And I'm sure you could probably say the same thing about yourself. I am not blaming my past and I am not encouraging you to do that either. My point is only to show you that as we grow up, we make choices and opinions about ourselves and others based on what we observe and experience. That's good news. It means we can continue to make choices, that is we can change based on what we learn now.

For example, I see how watching TV and the news made me question my environment as I grew up. When I watched the Brady Bunch, I thought that was the ultimate perfect family, and I knew my family was nothing like the Bradys. Of course, I was too young to realize there is no such thing as the perfect family.

Now, I realize that, while my family wasn't Brady Bunch perfect, everyone in it did the best they could. When my parents divorced, my mother suddenly became a single mom of a two-year-old, and two older boys. She also had a house to look after and no job. She did her best. I am proud of my mom and how hard she has worked to be the best mom she can be. After years of growing up, I finally realized that our parents do what they think is best. There is not one book with all the answers about how to raise happy, healthy children who are well adjusted and do not blame their parents for their lives. I am not blaming anyone. Rather, I am simply telling my story from my individual perspective. We all have our individual perspectives based on our ideas, thoughts, and memories, which we are entitled to. We get to own it.

On the positive side, TV also gave me an ideal to look up to: a strong, independent woman. To this day, I still love *The Mary Tyler Moore Show*, *That Girl*, and *One Day at a Time* because all the main characters were formidable women.

Similar to the TV role models, I had some amazing real life examples of strong women and how to have wonderful healthy relationships with women. My mom was a strong role model. She would always tell me to be independent and have my own bank account. I also learned about how to be a good mom from my mother. She worked throughout my entire childhood, took care of the house, and had what seemed to be a nice marriage with my dad.

And remember my friend, Sharyn? We are still supportive, strong friends. She is always there for me, and I am always there for her. My friends have always been an integral part of my life. Without them, I would not be the strong person I am today. We all need friends that will cheer us on, love us, and make sure we do not fall.

Unfortunately, not all the legacies of my childhood were as positive and empowering as my female role models. My story is more or less about men, and my ongoing desire to attract their attention with the greater hope that one day I would find one to love me. That desire obviously stems from my father leaving when I was such a young child.

Now I understand my biological father did what he thought was best and stayed out of our lives. His decision was not about me; it was about him, and what he was capable of. He died when I was sixteen years old. I never had the chance to have a relationship with him. But I did know people who knew him, and I would hear all the time how much I reminded them of him. I loved when people would tell me about him. My uncle was his best friend. After he died, my uncle asked me what I wanted to know about him. I did not know where to begin. I have had created a picture in my head of who he was. I had struggled for years to understand why he was incapable of loving my brothers and me.

I will never know the answer. However, I can tell you that I don't need to know anymore like I once did. This is because I have finally learned to live in the present. Presently, I love myself enough to say it was his decision, and we can never change the past. We can only learn from the past and live in the present.

I get it now. Everyone makes his or her own decisions, the best decision at the time. No one has a crystal ball and knows where their decision will lead them. This is why we all need to learn how to rely on ourselves. We need to learn to love ourselves through and through, and realize that we are who we are based on experiences throughout our lives. This is not a death sentence. It's a fact. And guess what? The good news is that we can change our lives. We have the power to create the life we want.

I am proof.

Chapter Two:
Two Marriages, Two Divorces, Too Many Bad Relationships

I tried marriage twice. And let's just say, it's not for me. One thing I am absolutely certain about: marriage is not for everyone. I think I have what I'd like to call "relationship ADD." I guess I haven't met a man who can keep my attention, which means I just haven't met the right one, yet.

In my twenties, all I wanted to do was get married. Okay, that's not the truth, I remember when I was in college saying: "All I want to do is get married and have children."

Now, as an adult who has been married and divorced twice, I know why I wanted to get married so badly. There are people who take time to think about the pros or cons when they make a decision in life. Not me. I really didn't stop to think about my life until recently. Like many people, I was predisposed to the idea that marriage and children would complete me. I'll even take that one step further and say that I *believed* my partner would complete me. I believed that walking down the aisle meant I was finally walking down the road to happiness.

Well we all know there is no actual road to happiness. There is, however, a way to happiness, and that way is through self-love and good, healthy self-esteem. But I didn't have that figured out before I got married. And as it turned out, walking down the aisle took me down a long and painful road.

I am sharing this part of my story to try to help anyone who may need a fresh perspective. I know about settling and being in bad relationships. Looking back now, my bad relationships were the best thing that ever happened to me because that was when I discovered I needed to change ME! It took me a very long time to realize that we can only control who we become and how we react to situations and people.

My first husband was emotionally and physically abusive to me. The first time he was abusive, I made an excuse for him. I remember saying that he didn't mean it, and he was tired. I was defending his behavior. Now, after years of therapy, I know why I was doing it. I wanted so badly to have the perfect family. I wanted to be married, raise children, and live happily ever after. I tried to convince myself that the first situation was an anomaly and it would never happen again. That he would never intentionally hurt me.

But he did.

It happened out of pure frustration. We were having problems. He had just lost his business and began changing—not for the better. One day, when I didn't see it coming, he grabbed me, held me by my throat, and threatened to hit me. I thought he was going to severely hurt me. I screamed, told him to get off me, and then I looked up and saw my four-year-old son watching us. I jumped up, grabbed my son, Jacob, and left.

That day was one of the most painful days in my life. I knew right then, that day would have an impact on Jacob. An impact that only he will ever truly know. I wanted to protect my son from the pain of an angry father. Although his father was never angry with Jacob, he was angry at how his own life had turned out, and he blamed everyone else.

In my mind, that was the last day I was married to my first husband, and I never looked back. After a nasty divorce, I was free. Free from emotional and physical abuse. The lasting impression on my psyche served as a reinforcement on my theme of not being good enough to be treated the way I deserved to be treated. I knew his treatment and behavior was not right at all, it simply made me feel less than and it was another reminder that I was not good enough.

My second marriage was a chemistry-free marriage. What I mean by that is we never had a burning desire to be physical together. We were friends and we forced our relationship to be more. Note to anyone who is looking for a relationship: don't force it. I was so convinced at this point in my life that you could not get everything that I settled for a comfortable friendship. But I craved that missing chemistry. It ate away at me. And then, to top it off, we had financial stressors affect our marriage. Our marriage died. Similarly, I felt I was dying inside. Ending the marriage seemed to be the only way for me to survive emotionally.

After my second marriage did not work out, I decided I'd had enough of being married. I wanted to be loved so badly, but I could not figure out how to let it happen. Why? I know now it's because I didn't love myself. How in God's name could I allow someone to love me back? Here I was, in my forties, and I still did not feel worthy of love except from my children, whom I love unconditionally. It was, and continues to be, my goal that my children never doubt how much they are loved and adored, and that they have high self-esteem.

My relationship problems were not confined to happening only when I was married. During my second marriage, I had hired a personal trainer to help me get into shape and feel better about my personal appearance. My weight has always been up and down.

After working out with him, we became friends, and we created a dynamic of a codependent friendship. He took over my world for two years and was the master of manipulation of me when my marriage was falling apart. He was smart enough to recognize my desire to be loved, and he used my weaknesses against me. He used his unhappy past to evoke strong emotions, so I became empathetic toward him. He became like a third child of mine, always wanting my attention and my help. He always needed me and that felt good to the person I was at that time: a woman who always wanted more, needed more, and desired more attention from a man.

After being his friend and trying to make him happy at all costs, I eventually realized that no matter what I did for him, it would never be good enough. I would never be good enough. One day, I woke up feeling terrible about myself. I was so incredibly sad that I knew it was time to make a change, a real change, not something that I just talked about. But I wasn't sure how to do it or even what exactly needed to change. I decided to make a list, to catalogue events that made me unhappy to see if that could help me figure out what needed to change.

I created a Word document on my computer, and every time I would get into an argument or a fight with the trainer, whatever it was, I wrote it down. It was an ongoing document that was filled with unhappiness. He said some of the meanest things to me anyone has ever said. I was so comfortable in this pattern of wanting love that I was willing to do anything to make it work.

At one point, after reading over what I'd just written, I called a good friend and told her about a fight my trainer and I had gotten into. She asked: "Why are you working so hard to get him to love you?"

Man, did that hurt. The realization from that statement was so true and real, I could feel the pain in my heart and my gut. It was an emotional pain that made me physically sick. I realized I'd worked my whole life to have a man pay attention to me, love me, and make me feel relevant. After a very long time of adding to my unhappiness journal, I realized it was my responsibility to love me and make myself feel relevant. If I wanted to be happy and emotionally fulfilled, I would have to make the change. No one else could do it for me.

Finally, after spending a long weekend with him, I decided I'd had enough. I walked out of his house, and I never looked back. It was so hard. I kept telling myself that if I did not love me, no one else would. If I did not walk away, he was going to kill me emotionally. I had lost who I was. I was in the darkest place of my life. I was allowing myself to be treated poorly because I did not value who I was. I was so incredibly empty at that point. It was such a lonely place to be.

I pretended to be fine for the sake of my boys. Inside I was suffering from years of pent-up unhappiness. I cried in the shower so my boys would not hear me. I cried when I was alone in my car. I could not stop crying. It wasn't just over him that I was crying. I was crying because I wanted to be loved and valued so badly that I had allowed myself to be treated so poorly, only to end up still wanting love.

Eventually, I had cried enough and reached a place where I knew I needed to break that cycle of negative relationships.

Today, I refer to this person as the best thing that ever happened to me. Because of him, and the emotional abuse I sustained from him, I was able to look at my life, my behavioral and relationship patterns, and say *enough*!

I did not realize at the time what a long journey it would be to heal. It was three of the most intensive years of my life. They were filled with struggle, loneliness, and pain. And I had to sit with it. Sitting with your feelings is not easy. It's exhausting. But coming out on the other side makes it all worthwhile.

Neither of my marriages ended in a "happily ever after" style. That's because "happily ever after" does not exist.

As I have grown and learned to appreciate myself and my own strengths as an adult, I now want to help others see that being married can be a beautiful part of life, but it is truly not the answer to finding happiness or being complete. Here's the deal. Getting married and having children are not for everyone. It wasn't for me. The getting married part was, but not the staying married part.

The gift I got from both my marriages ending was a valuable lesson: in order to bounce back from anything, including broken marriages, you MUST know where you want to bounce to. What I mean is, you must stop and think: figure out what you want your life to be like, figure out where you want to go.

In order for me to bounce back from bad relationships, I had to understand my behavioral patterns and the way I thought, so that I could understand exactly what I needed and was looking for in a mate.

Here is what does exist: if you are lucky, really lucky, you will find someone whom you can love unconditionally, and who loves you. Just like with any relationship or friendship in your lifetime, you have to be willing to commit to a long road of ups and downs. I think finding the right partner is possible, but I do believe many people get married to the wrong partner for the wrong reasons.

I hear it all the time from young adults, mostly women: "I cannot wait to graduate, so I can get married." They are in a hurry to get married, buy a house, have children, buy a bigger house, and on and on it goes.

But, here is my question to YOU and to anyone who is struggling with not being married at this point in his or her life: Why do so many people believe that if they get married and have children, their life will suddenly, automatically, almost magically be perfect?

No one shares these following truths with you when you are thinking about getting married and building the "perfect family."

1. There is no such thing as a perfect family. It simply does not exist.
2. Marriage does not complete you or make you happy. If you are not happy when you get married, what makes you think you will be happy after marriage?
3. No one really asks whether this is the person who will grow with you through better and worse, sickness and health.

Think about this: if you are in your twenties, you will continue to grow and change. What happens if your partner does not?

I am not cynical at all about marriage. I think if you want it, great. Just be realistic. I know that no one wants to listen because everyone believes that the partner they are with at this very moment is the forever one. We think that way because we are raised to believe that. Throughout my career, I have worked with, and continue to mentor, a lot of young women in their twenties who are bright and beautiful. And almost every one of them has getting married on their to-do list.

With both my marriages, I glossed over some things about my husbands-to-be that I shouldn't have. I told myself those things wouldn't bother me after we were married because they'd change. WRONG!

So, as I bounced back from my divorces, I finally stopped to think about what I MUST HAVE in a relationship. Here is my list:

1. Likes and is good with kids.
2. Smart.
3. Funny.
4. Good character, including loyalty.
5. Has good chemistry with me.

Do you have a list of core values you are looking for in a mate? Is your current relationship meeting your expectations? If you are thinking about marriage, my recommendation is that you take the time to stop, think, and ask yourself: does this person have the core values I am looking for in a life partner?

> **Let me tell you this: the thing that annoys you the most about your partner today will always annoy you. You cannot change anyone but yourself, so do not think you will change your partner or spouse. And I'm not just talking about what annoys you; I'm talking about all your future spouse's habits. I remember being at a wedding shower and a girl was telling me how her friend was planning to marry someone who struggled with an alcohol problem. She said that her friend did not seem to realize that the alcohol problem would still be there after they got married. That's exactly right. Remember this: when you marry a person who has things about him or her that you do not like, chances are the person is not going to change.**

The desire to be loved and accepted never goes away. You get this nagging pain inside of you because you know there is something missing. So you can see how my early childhood desire to be loved and accepted continued and intensified when I was an adult. What I now realize is that I could never feel loved and accepted until I learned to love and accept myself and that it's impossible to have a healthy relationship with a man (or anyone else) until I can have that relationship with me.

It took me lots of hard work, the desire to change, and buckets of tears to figure out how to love and accept myself. But I did it. Now I'm happier than I ever dreamed possible. I did it with my 4-step plan as outlined in the following section.

Section 2
The 4-Step
Bounce Back
Into You!
Plan

Chapter Three:
Step One – Get Clarity

As I grew up and for a long while as an adult, I wore one-way, rose-colored glasses. For some reason, those glasses prevented me from seeing the good inside me and yet they encouraged me to believe that everyone else was good, and that no one had a bad intention.

Now, my glasses see everything in a lightly rose-colored fashion. My oldest son Jacob often tells me, "Mom, you always see the good in people." It's true. I did, and still do, because I believe we all have good in us. But that doesn't mean that every person we meet is good for us.

I have learned to pay close attention to the "energy" surrounding me when I am with other people. As you can probably guess after reading about my college years and marriages, there were many times when I said to myself, "something doesn't feel right." How many times have you said that? I have said it a lot. And guess what? Inevitably, every time I say that to myself, it's true.

Yet, so many of us have trained ourselves not to trust our gut. We tend to over think our feelings or we try to make the situation right and usually we fail. Take it from me, when and if something does not feel right, please do not try to make it work. In the end, it won't last. From my experiences, when there is a feeling, or an energy, that is uncomfortable, there is a reason for it.

So what should you do when your gut is telling you something is wrong? You should get clarity about the situation. And you should do the same thing when your gut never even bothers to give you a hint about something and yet you wound up in a negative place. Before you can leave a situation, before you can make a change to the circumstances, you have to figure out exactly why it happened in the first place. Otherwise, you risk repeating the situation or finding yourself in a worse one. Because when you get clarity, you often discover your problems really stem from beliefs you hold about yourself and your life.

Getting clarity means you stop and think about the situations where you're unhappy. You ask yourself some tough questions about it. And then you identify the specific elements, the beliefs, that are at the root of the issues. In other words, getting clarity means you do a situational analysis to find the root cause of your unhappiness.

Here are some questions to get you started:

- What specific areas in your life are making you unhappy? Career? Marriage? Parenting? School? Friendships or other relations?
- Within those specific areas, can you identify specific people or incidents that truly bring on negative feelings within you?
- Can you name the feelings? That is, can you specifically identify the emotional nature of your unhappiness? Is it fear? Anger? Worry? Frustration?
- Looking back over your past, can you identify if or when you were in similar situations? Is there anything repetitive or cyclical going on?
- Do you feel responsible for the situation?
- Do you feel you deserve to be unhappy?

If, when you're asking yourself these questions, you think something like: *This is dumb. These questions are no-brainers. I don't have to think about them,"* then you're not digging deep enough inside yourself.

Let me give you an example of what I mean by digging deep inside yourself with an example of when I had to get clarity in a situation.

After declaring personal bankruptcy and my second divorce was final, I started my marketing business, which meant I had to network and meet a lot of new people. Prior to that, most of my career was based in Philadelphia. I had lived and worked there my entire life. I had plenty of contacts and I knew enough people to know that I was never really surrounded by strangers in the business world. Networking in Philly was easy and comfortable for me.

However, I started my new business in New Jersey, where no one knew me and where I needed to make a name for myself. The fear was overwhelming. I was constantly running and gunning, trying to keep my too few new clients happy, struggling through the growing pains of a start-up business, and doing my best to be a good mom for my boys. I literally lived in total fear for the first year of my business.

Here's the crazy thing, though I knew I was scared, I just didn't take the time to stop and think about what was at the root of the fear.

Eventually, I did. Yes, on the surface, it was obvious: I was scared my new business might fail. But when I dug a little deeper, I realized that if it did fail, I could always go back to work in the corporate world, so becoming destitute wasn't the real issue. The real issue was that I was scared to death of failing because I believed that if I failed with my business, then that would mean I was a failure too. In other words, I believed my worth as a human being was dependent on whether or not a marketing company succeeded.

After I realized where all my energy had been going–to prove that I meant something because I was a successful woman–I was able to re-channel it to where I wanted it to be: on me feeling confident and secure. Which meant I had to become confident and secure. I knew I was good at marketing. There was no need to worry about proving that. What I needed to do was prove I was good at being me.

I started networking with the sole purpose of giving people in Jersey a chance to meet me, Lisa. Not just the head of a marketing firm. Soon enough I met a very special woman named Penny at a networking event. She approached me and said, "Lisa, I love your hair." My hair is unique, to say the least. I wear it big, curly, and red, and it has become something of an accessory for me. People notice it, and it makes for a great conversation starter, as it did with Penny. We spoke for several minutes and I got a wonderful vibe from her, so I agreed to meet again for coffee. Remember, she was a stranger, and we had just met.

I'm so glad I listened to my gut when it told me Penny was someone I needed to meet. Over coffee, she said, "I will introduce you to the people you need to know." And she did! She would e-mail or call me and say, "You need to know this person." Penny opened doors for me, and I will always remember her generosity, and continue to move it forward in her honor. But she only opened the doors for me because I opened the door to me first to her.

> **Even after starting a business and getting my master's, I continue to be educated on a daily basis not only about business but on the kind of people who do and don't feel right for me to be around. We live in a fast-paced world where we are easily connected to people via social media. We are constantly "meeting" people through Facebook, LinkedIn and many other impersonal outlets. It's very difficult to get a feel for people when we never meet them in person. But you should never stop listening to your gut and assessing your life. I encourage you to make the same habit I have made to stop and ask *Does this feel right?* as you go through your day-to-day life.**

Get Clarity Exercises

1. Ask questions! As I said, asking yourself some tough questions and forcing yourself to go deeper than the surface answers is the first step in getting clarity. Here's an example about going deeper with a woman named Polly.

What is making Polly unhappy?
> Her first answer: "I hate my job."

What specific elements about her job does she hate?
> "Lots! My boss constantly requests me to work late. While I like the extra money, by working late I can't pick up my son from day care at the normal time, so that extra money I make is spent on paying to have him stay late. And then we get home even later, so all we have time is for dinner, to get him bathed and tucked in. I feel like I don't get any fun time with him. Also, I don't feel comfortable around most of my coworkers. They're all a bunch of catty, gossipy women who don't like me. And also, my cubicle is a depressing gray color."

Digging deeper, Polly starts to name the feelings she feels when she's at work.

> Regarding her boss, the first emotion she names is frustration. But when she thinks about why she's frustrated, she realizes she feels as if her boss doesn't respect her time outside of work. That he doesn't respect her as a human being.

> Similarly, when she thinks about her catty coworkers, she realizes she feels insecure around them, as if they are judging her negatively and that they don't respect her.

> And when she thinks about the gray cubicle being depressing, she wonders why she doesn't do anything to change it, like add posters or bring in flowering plants. When she thinks on it, her initial reaction is "It's not worth it," which she realizes means "I'm not worth it."

> By digging deeper, Polly realizes it's her own feelings of not being worthy of respect that make her feel unable to explain her daycare situation to her boss and that also make her feel uncomfortable around her coworkers.

> When Polly thinks back over her past, she realizes at previous jobs,

during her school years, and even in her former marriage, she experienced similar circumstances. She discovers she needs to learn to respect herself if she is ever to receive the respect of others. We'll re-visit Polly later in the book.

2. Create a "Get Clarity Journal." Keep a notepad handy and throughout the course of your day, every day, note down times when you feel unhappy in some way. At the end of the day, go over your notes and see what common elements are at the root of your unhappiness by asking yourself the Get Clarity questions above. Think on each question and answer. Make sure you're getting to the absolute truth, the clarity, for each one.

    When I first did this process, I discovered there were three main underlying issues I needed to tackle:
    - How to identify what I needed and wanted in a healthy relationship with a man.
    - How to learn to create boundaries with people.
    - How to learn to say *no*.

    As with Polly's story, we'll revisit these issues soon to see living proof of how it all works together.

3. Nightly Exercises: As you read through this book, you'll notice that I recommend taking some time every night to write in a journal. For the Step One process, each night take some time to assess your day. Think about how you handled different situations, about what worked and what didn't work. Be honest and admit when you were kind and respectful, when you were not, and whether you were consistent in your use of good judgment.

    Periodically, leaf back through your journal and take stock of your answers. You may discover you're engaging in patterns of behavior that are more hurtful than helpful. You may also discover areas where you are stuck and not moving forward. Take those areas and ask the Get Clarity questions, go deep into them and discover what you can change about yourself to create a happier, healthier you.

By taking the time to get clear, you will be able to identify exactly what is not working in your life and the beliefs about yourself that are at the root of it all. By doing that, you will be able to work toward changing the situations to make them better. That almost sounds like the next step would be about how to make that change, right? Well, it's not. There are another couple of steps to go through before we can actually make the plans to change.

Right now, the next step, Step Two of my Four-step Bounce Back Into You plan, is to Get Real.

Chapter 4:
Step Two – Get Real

The subtitle for this chapter and step could be: "What's your responsibility here?"

Let's face it, the only person you can ever really change is yourself. We all know this and yet we still try to make our kids be who we want them to be in order for us to be happy. How many times have you heard (or even said yourself) something like: "If only my husband wasn't so irritable, I'd be in a more stable marriage." Or, "If I only I was twenty pounds lighter, I'd be happy." Or, if only my boss wasn't a tyrant, I'd like my job." So part of getting real is discovering and admitting the truths behind your "if only" statements.

Using Polly's example in the previous chapter, we can see that if her boss and coworkers had been more sensitive, she'd be happier at work. And if her cubicle wasn't gray, she'd find it more pleasant to be in.

However, if she were to get real, she would realize if she had treated herself with the respect she demanded from others, the first time her boss asked her to work late, she would have explained her home situation to him and then offered to work out another solution to get the job done without sacrificing time with her son and money out of her pocket. If she had treated herself with respect from day one, she wouldn't value the opinions of other people over her own, so she wouldn't care what the catty coworkers thought of her.

But getting real isn't just about stopping the blame game. It's also about taking stock of the relationships and habits you have that put you in unhappy situations.

By getting real about your friendships and relationships, you are forced to get real with your part in those relationships. You are forced to admit whether the person you're presenting to the world is your authentic self (or not). And it also forces you to admit your role in unhealthy relationships so that you can change them for the better or end them, if necessary.

I remember when I decided that my friend who used to be the girlfriend I could not live without, no longer was the girl I thought she was. Then I realized it was not the friend who had changed, it was me. And what had happened was quite simple: growth. We had grown in two different directions.

For me, the more I grew up, the less I needed other people to approve of me. I no longer needed people to okay my outfit, my decisions, my behavior, or lifestyle. I started to trust my own gut. The more I trusted my own gut, the more I realized my friend had always tried to control me and I had always let her. I wasn't happy in a controlling friendship, yet I had allowed it to happen. By getting real, by taking responsibility for my part in the relationship, I redefined our friendship and changed the way we related to each other to be more positive and healthy.

FRIENDS ARE THE FLOWERS OF LIFE

I now think of my life as a beautiful bouquet with lots of different types of flowers. The flowers come in different colors, textures, and shapes. Together or separately, they add beauty to the world. Well, I have a beautiful bouquet of friends.

We are all like a beautiful bouquet with all different colors representing different pieces of what makes each one of us "us." In my bouquet, the brightest colors speak to my vibrant personality. The red ones are my energy and passion to help people see their inner beauty and embrace it. The greenery is the calm, the mainstay of the bouquet. For me, the calm is my children.

Think about the most beautiful bouquet of flowers, and picture it. Go ahead, picture what your bouquet looks like. What flowers represent your beauty?

We all have our own personal beauty, and we all add something to make the world a more beautiful place, separately or together. Maybe, the next time you look at someone, you will remember they are wearing a mask. They are hiding their pain, their insecurity, their low self-esteem, or whatever it is. Everyone is hiding behind a mask.

If you decide to take the time to see what is beneath the mask, then maybe you will begin to see their beauty.

Getting real can be painful and scary because sometimes it means that, if you truly are committed to living the happiest life you can, then you have to break off relationships or drastically change the dynamics of your life. But think about this: Every season we clean out our closets. We decide what we are going to keep because we just cannot live without it, and then we decide what we are going to donate because for some reason, it's just not working for us anymore. So I ask the following: Why would we not do that with our friends? Our health habits? Our career strategies? Our lives?

Yes, getting real can be difficult and painful in the short term, but the end results—a happy you!—are well worth it.

Get Real Exercises

1. Examine the people in your life. Do you surround yourself with individuals who love and support you as your truest self? The truth is that you can accomplish so much by trusting, loving, and accepting yourself; however, an important part of bouncing back is having a strong support system of people who believe in you and the goodness you carry inside.

2. Create your ideal team lineup. I am the manager of my team of friends and family. Your team should be made up of people who love and support you. If you're at this step and you think to yourself, "I don't have many people on my side," don't despair. Put together your lineup as best you can. You will discover as you Bounce Back Into You and become an authentically happy and confident person, you will attract the right people to you to be on your team. Remember, though, not everyone needs to play on your team.

    As you think about your team, ask yourself who your catcher would be. Who is the one person who is always there to catch you when you feel you might fall? Who is your first baseman, the first person you turn to when you need to vent or cry? Who are your cheerleaders? Who can play the role of umpire and help you see another person's point of view?

    The point of this exercise is to realize that although each of your friends has special, unique qualities, they all should have supporting and loving roles in your life. If you find yourself on a team where everyone is a coach or manager and you are the bat boy, then you must realize you're taking a very inactive role in leading your life.

    If the baseball analogy doesn't work for you, perhaps try using a live performance instead for this exercise. There are players on the stage, supporting players, background technicians, and audience members in the orchestra seats, middle section, balcony and box seats. When I tried this exercise for the first time on myself, I realized I was surrounded by people

41

in the orchestra seats. Up close and personal. It was exhausting having everyone so close. I discovered I needed to grow a little distance for us all to be able to breathe with ease.

3. Nighttime journaling. This is going to sound odd, but hear me out. Take some time to journal a note of thanks to all the people who have taught you lessons of exactly how you do not want to be. If the cashier was rude to you at the market, thank him or her for the reminder that we should never punish other people because we ourselves are tired or stressed. If someone at work behaved in a passive-aggressive way, thank him or her for the reminder that everyone benefits from an open and honest workplace.

    Some of my greatest adversaries have taught me some of my greatest life lessons. I stop and think about these people frequently and what they have shown me by being a poor example. I love to observe the people around me. I am a student of people, and it's fascinating to watch how some of them operate. If you can emotionally step back in situations and observe people in action, often you'll discover that they are not mean but are scared and defensive. They are not backstabbers, but are insecure. Those are the lessons to learn from negative people.

So now that you've finished the first two steps, you should be clear about the core beliefs you hold about yourself that are at the root of your problems and you should also have an idea of what your role or responsibility is in the negative situations in your life. You're still not ready to put a plan of action together, though. First you need to stop and think about what you want your life to be like. You have to do that first, so that you can then plan the right course of action to attain it. In Step Three, Get Vision, you figure out what you want your life to be like.

Chapter Five:
Step 3 – Get Vision

Hopefully the first two steps have helped you figure something out: you get to create your life. That's right. The way you think and the choices you make really do create your life.

How cool is that?

Because knowing that, knowing that you create your life, means you now know you get to create your *ideal* life. So once again stop and think. What does your ideal life look like? What is the best version of you?

That second question might be hard for you to answer right now. It's very possible that you, like many of us, have no idea of what the best version of yourself looks like. That's because many of us wear masks so much, that we're not sure who our authentic selves really are.

I believe everyone wears a mask at some point in their lives. Some people wear them all the time. It's when you wear them too much (or all the time) that you create problems for yourself and you put yourself in situations where you don't want to be.

> **When I was young, I remember looking out the window of my home and watching a young couple make out. (Oh, I hope I am not dating myself with that term. Do kids still call it that?) I turned to my mom and said, "Look how happy they look."**
>
> **My mom offered me some really good advice. She said, "Lisa, you never really know what someone, or a couple, is going through."**
>
> **Remember, things are never what they appear to be on the outside. What a powerful message, and how true it is.**

Think about two or three people that you know today. Think about what they project to the world. Do they seem overly confident? Are they really *that* confident? A couple of my favorite sayings are "don't believe the hype" and "look beyond the mask."

I bet if someone took a survey about how many people believe they are truly showing the world who they really are, most people would say they do not show their true self. And then they'd make excuses to justify why. I know I did. I used to tell myself that I could not be as nice as I really am because then people would take advantage of me. I lived protecting myself, to avoid being vulnerable and getting hurt. I will admit it was hard to even type the word vulnerable. After all, why would anyone want to make him or herself vulnerable?

Ooo, the BIG V! That's what my old friend Lori and I used to call *vulnerability*. When we met, Lori and I were both wearing our masks to protect ourselves from being hurt. It had happened repeatedly in the past, so how could we believe that anything would be different? And yet, when we both took the time to look beyond the mask and get to know each other, we were rewarded by being able to become true, authentic friends.

And yet I continued to wear the mask in front of others. I wore it so much, I didn't even realize it was on half the time. My dear friend Sheri had to point it out to me. We used to spend a lot of time talking in person, the good old-fashioned way, at our kitchen tables. I swear one day we will write a book called "Kitchen Talk," and it will be all about our talks over salads and what we have learned from each other. Anyway, one day, she leaned across the table and said, "Bien," that is what she calls me when she is serious, "I had lunch with so-and-so the other day, and they don't really know the real you. Why don't you show people who you really are?"

Hmm...good question. And so I set to task at chipping away at my mask to eventually show the world who I really am. I had worn a mask for most of my life. I had pretended to be confident. I had pretended to have conviction when I made any decision, even when I was steeped in self-doubt. Who am I kidding? It wasn't *when* I was steeped in self-doubt! I was always in self-doubt. I was riddled with it. Jeesh, but it feels great today to really show the world who I am. I am a loving, kind, funny, passionate woman who accepts who she is and is not afraid to show the world.

But it wasn't easy. To take off the mask, I had to work through the stuff that created it.

> We all have to work through our "stuff." We all have a story about who we are and what our lives are like. That's where the "stuff" comes from: the events we experience, the people we spend time with, the beliefs we embrace, etc. Some people stay on the surface with their "stuff" – they only talk about it, usually talk and complain about it, a lot. Others stay on the surface with their "stuff," but instead of complaining about it, they believe they are perfect just the way they are and nothing needs to change. They are all wearing a mask.

Remember when I mentioned being the tallest girl in class and the bad haircut that resulted in my being nicknamed Bird's Nest Bien? So now you know I felt odd, unattractive and not good enough in school. As if that weren't enough, I also developed a personal "you-are-not-smart-enough" mantra, too. That belief began in fifth grade when my teacher was trying hard to help me understand long division. Eventually, he put his hands over his face, shook his head, and asked, "What don't you understand?"

My family also tried to help me understand long division. I just could not get it. How old are you when you are in fifth grade—ten or eleven? Such a long time ago for me and yet that memory still is in my mind.

Math. Dreaded math!

Math homework for me was a family affair. First my mom would try to help. Then one of my brothers would try. And then, if we were really stuck, we would wait for my dad because he was really good in math and always knew the answer. I was always amazed how easy it was for him, let alone everyone else, but not for me. I hated that I wasn't good in math.

"Don't worry, Lisa, you don't have to be good in math. I was not good in math either," is what my mom would say.

Once again, I am not blaming anyone, I am sharing stories that I think will resonate with others. I want to show that when we are young, we hear what people say. And then we often don't have the maturity and skill set to decide if, in fact, what they say is true. I internalized the reaction from my teacher and questioned my mother's response. Was it really okay that I was not good at math? Did that mean I wasn't as smart as everyone else?

So began the message: YOU ARE NOT SMART ENOUGH AND NOT PRETTY ENOUGH!

In school, there were always the really smart kids, the kids who needed extra help, and then the rest who fell in between. Obviously, as far as math went, I was one who needed extra help, but for the rest my subjects, I was somewhere in between. So I figured school was not for me. When it was time to decide what track to pursue for high school, I told my brother I was not going to pursue the college path, after all I had been donning a mask that "not smart enough" kids wear. We didn't go to college. He insisted I was making a mistake. He wanted me to take courses that would prepare me for college. It was his belief in me that allowed me to even consider it.

Needing to raise my GPA, I attended community college prior to applying to a four-year institution. After community college, I applied to Temple University in Philadelphia, was accepted, and graduated with a GPA equivalent to a B+. It was at Temple that my belief that I was not smart enough changed. One professor nominated me for an award, and miraculously to me, I won! I will never forget when she told me that I won. I felt as if I had finally made it. I *was* smart enough. I even had evidence.

But just because I was smart in school, didn't mean that I felt smart all the time. However, I did switch masks and wore one where I pretended to be smart.

In 2010, I was forced to start my own business. The economy was really bad, which I am sure you all know, but my children needed to eat. I started B!EN Marketing Group, and I was so scared. I lived in constant fear that clients would think I was not smart enough to do the job they hired me for. Every day, and I mean every day, I put on my mask and told myself, "little Lisa in my head will not mess with me. I am smart enough."

And, then, someone said to me, "Lisa, listen to the evidence, listen to the evidence."

Evidence I get is when my clients say things like: "Wow Lisa! Your assessment of the situation is right on." Or "Lisa, your idea was brilliant!"

I am still listening even to this day. The evidence is real. It allowed me to take off my mask. Actually, to even see it, I had to take it off because when I acknowledged that my client was right, when I see the proof that my idea worked, I can't help but admit *I am smart enough!*

Your evidence will be different for you. It could be how your ideas created sales for the company you work for. It could be that your cupcakes won an award for being the best in the region. Evidence is proof of the real you—not what you *think* is the real you. It's proof you can use to stop your negative thinking.

I know I am not alone when it comes to hearing tired, negative voices from childhood in my head. We all have self-doubt, regardless of whether we created our own perceptions of who we are or if others helped along the way. And many of us feel the need to hide that self-doubt behind a mask of "it's all good here" instead of dealing with it.

I'm here to tell you, though, that you have to drop your mask if you are going to create the life of your dreams. You can't pretend happiness into happening. You have to allow yourself to actually be happy. So, the first part of creating your vision, then, is to start finding the evidence of your skills, your knowledge, your passion, your creativity, your special you-ness.

The second part of creating your vision comes from learning to separate who you really are from your situations in life. That is, by not defining yourself based on what's going on with you.

Let me explain with another story from my life. The day I walked out of the bankruptcy attorney's office was one of the worst in my life. I cried and cried, then I cried some more.

I had always been financially responsible and proud of my high credit rating. I felt like a failure. But I had no other option but to file it. While meeting with my dear friend who is an accountant, he had turned to me and said, "You are left with no choice."

Sometimes in life, it's that simple. You have no other decision.

So there I was, a single mom of two boys. I was broke and unemployed. But I was so very lucky because I had people everywhere I turned trying to help me, support me, and love me. Sometimes though, when going through a hard time, some of us have a tendency to push people away and not ask for help. It's not the smartest course of action, but we do it because we allow our pride to get in the way. The truth is sometimes we let our ego get the best of us and for me, when I filed bankruptcy that was exactly what I did. I was too proud to tell anyone. It was so embarrassing to me. To this day, I still haven't shared this story with all the supportive people close to me. As you read this and learn about this hard time and how I overcame it, so will my family and friends.

Looking back, I realize why my pride stood in the way. It took me a long time to accept the fact that the bankruptcy did not define me, that the bankruptcy was something that had *happened* to me. It wasn't something that I had become. In other words, the bankruptcy was not the REAL me. I was still Lisa, the kind person with a good heart. I had just gotten stuck in a bad financial situation.

As my accountant friend had explained, the government has the bankruptcy solution in place to help people get back on their feet. In other words, it was created to help people bounce back financially. So as I slowly figured out that the bankruptcy was something I was going through, that it had nothing to do with who I was as an individual, I also realized that it could be a stepping-stone, another launching pad for me to bounce back. In other words, it was an event that I could make something good come from.

And bounce back is what I did. In 2010, I started my own marketing and communications business. It has not been easy. I repeat, it has not been easy. I continue to learn more and more about being an entrepreneur, but mostly I continue to learn what I am capable of, what the real me is capable of.

> One of my first exercises after starting my business was to create a daily checklist. Have you ever done that? It's a great way to stay on track.
>
> Here was my checklist the day I started my business:
>
> ✓ Be committed, not just interested.
> ✓ Move it forward every day!
> ✓ Learn to live with the discomfort.
> ✓ Remember how you do anything is how you do everything!
> ✓ Pay attention to everyone you are speaking to.
> ✓ Make a list of five target customers, review who they are, call them!
> ✓ Be a lifelong learner committed to growth!

So, drop your mask, accept who the authentic you is and realize you're not your situations. Those are the required elements to have in place before you can Get Vision and define what you want your life to be like. And to do that, here are a few exercises.

Exercises

1. Imagine your ideal life every night. Close your eyes every night before you go to bed and picture who you want to be. I picture every piece of my life: my health and looks, my career, my relationships, everything. We become what we think about good, bad, and ugly. So take the time to really think about what the best life would be for you. Write in your journal how you feel in your best life. Do you feel energized? Relaxed? Eager? Steady? Confident?

2. Nightly exercise: every night as you write in your journal, make a point to

complete the following prompts:

- In six months, I want to be _____
- In one year, I want to be _____
- In five years, I want to be _____

Identify the trends in your dreams and goals, let them vary naturally as you start to discover what your true aims and intentions are in life.

3. Take the blinders off. This is probably the toughest exercise and maybe even the most painful. But you will get soooooo much out of it.

   Make a list of what you think are your strengths and weaknesses.

   Next, ask your closest friends and family members to help you by participating in an informal "focus group." Tell them, for example, "I want to know why you like our friendship/relationship or what you get out of it." And then when you meet up, ask some hard questions. Here are a few to get you started:

   - "Do you think I am too picky or judgmental?"
   - "Am I hard on you?"
   - "Do you think I'm hard on myself?"
   - "How would you describe my average mood?"
   - "How well do you think I handle problems or conflicts?"
   - "How do you describe my style of communication?"

   Whatever their answer, trust yourself that you want to know it and that you are unafraid of their honesty. (And when you think about it, there's no reason to be afraid because we are only asking the people we consider our friends, advocates, and mentors who have our best interests at heart.) Write down what you learned from those you trust most in your life. And then ask each one to tell you what he or she thinks is one of your better qualities, your most positive aspects. Make a list of those, as well, and add it to your of strengths (number 3 above). After the group leaves, compare and contrast your list with the one you created from your focus group. Can you identify where you wear a mask instead of allowing yourself to be the real you?

   As you compare and contrast the lists, think on the relationships or situations in your life that are not working. Can you determine what role you are playing in those relationships or situations? Are you playing that role or is it your mask?

Now you know the beliefs that are at the root of your negative situations, you know what your role and responsibilities are in them, and you have an idea of what your ideal life should be like. It's finally time to put together a plan to help you combine everything you've learned to get that happy life you so deserve.

Chapter 6:
Step 4 – Get Going!

You're finally there!

Now you have clarity: you know what beliefs you hold about yourself that are putting you in and keeping you in negative situations.

Now you have a real, definite sense of responsibility for your choices and thoughts and you understand your role in your problems and your relationships.

And now you know what you want your life to look like.

So all that's left is to put it all together and create the change you want to create.

We're all familiar with goal setting, so what I suggest you do now will probably be something you know how to do: Create a Life Map! Basically, a life map says: "I am here. I want to be there. Here is how I plan to do it." And then you write down the steps

In Step Three, one of the exercises was to journal each night in order to help you define what you want your life to look like. Review those notes and become as specific as possible about what each goal is that you want set in order to create the change you want in your life.

Take a big, poster board and use markers to map out your dreams. Start by thinking logically about what is involved in getting it done. Break it down into steps. Do you want a new job? Well, first you have to decide what kind of job you want, what industry. Next you have to figure out if you have the right skills for it. If not, then you have to figure out how you will get the skills and where you will learn them. You will also need to think about your resume, cover letters, where you will search, what kinds of networking contacts you have, etc.

Map out the goal and the steps on your poster board. It may help if you begin with the end in mind and work backward. Just be sure to leave some blank space between each step for times of evaluation.

Here is part of my life map I made for this book, as an example. I had a poster board for this book on my office wall for a long while. Now, I am finally able to share my story as well as some exercises that helped me get my life headed in the direction I wanted to go.

My list for the book included:

- Research – Doing research about self-publishing versus finding a publisher.
- Editor/Publisher – Finding and selecting an editor/publisher
- Writing – I added writing in my schedule so that every night I had an hour or two to write available to me.
- Timeline – I created a timeline for myself, my designer and editor. We worked backward from the launch date we selected.

Included in my current life map and goals are the following:

- Developing and launching a successful YouTube Channel.
- Becoming a nationally recognized motivational speaker.
- Doing a TedTalk.
- And, of course, continuing with my series of Bouncing Back books. My next book is on bouncing back from divorce.

One thing to remember is that every plan needs evaluation. So, on your life map mark out periods of time for you to honestly assess your situation of where you are, what you learned since the last step and whether or not the future steps need to change.

Think about this part as if it's your personal accountability step. Throughout my journey, whenever I decide to make a change or create something new in my life, I always stop and ask myself: *How are you doing?* No one, and I mean no one, lives without a setback or two or three. We all have setbacks so throughout our journeys we have to stop and regroup. It's a natural part of the process.

But these evaluation points on your life map have another reason for being. Remember all that work you did in steps one, two and three? As you work toward your goals, as you focus on building the life of your dreams, you will probably be haunted by old habits.

During your evaluation times, as you assess, go back and revisit the journaling notes you took in StepOne. Are any of your old beliefs getting in the way of your new goals? Are you slipping back into negative patterns with your relationships that might prevent you from achieving your dreams? Are you putting on a mask to appear like you are someone you're not?

The thing is, when we realize we're not happy in a situation and we want to make a change, if it were as simple as setting a goal and taking the steps to get there, we'd all be achieving our goals on an ongoing basis. Unfortunately, the truth is, it's not that simple. And that's because, I believe, whether or not we bounce back from a negative situation is dependent on one thing and one thing alone: whether or not we love ourselves unconditionally.

Let's revisit Polly from Step One to help me explain.

Polly learned that, although she said she thought her problem was that she hated her job, the real reason she was unhappy was that she felt disrespected at work. Digging deeper, she realized the truth: she didn't feel worthy of being respected. Otherwise, she would have handled the situation with her boss differently from the very beginning. So while Polly could create a life map for changing jobs, she'll probably end up in a similar situation unless she changes herself. Likewise, before she can expect any changes to happen at work, she needs to make a change within herself if she is to ever feel respected. And that change, based on the best version of herself, would be to feel worthy of being respected. To feel confident and know she has value. All of which means, Polly must learn to love and accept herself unconditionally. Yes, at the root of Polly's problem at work is a lack of self-love!

And to revisit my lessons learned in Step One (identify what I needed and wanted in a healthy relationship with a man; learning to create boundaries, learning to say *no*), you'll see I discovered similar results. Digging deeper, I realized all three were all the same issue: I needed to create boundaries. When someone has difficulty creating boundaries in relationships, that's often a sign that that person doesn't value him or herself much. In other words, I needed to learn to love myself more. Yes, the root of my problems also comes back to self-love!

Does that mean no life maps should be created? Not at all. It just means to create them with open eyes. Create them for what your best vision of yourself is and work toward them as best you can, but always remember:

You cannot fully bounce back from any situation

Unless you bounce back into you!

You have to learn to love yourself in order to bounce back successfully.

I'm ending this chapter with a few exercises to help you stay motivated while you follow your life maps. In the next section, I share some tips and techniques to help you have the greatest love affair of all: with yourself!

Get Going Exercises

1. Use Post It! Notes (my favorites!). Write some of the positive comments about your strengths that your Focus group gave you back in Step Three on Post It! notes and stick them in places you will see them frequently. Read them before you speak with people at work. Before you make difficult phone calls. Put them on your mirror and read them while you brush your teeth and groom each day. Stick them on the cupboard above the coffeepot and read them when your pour a cup each morning.

2. Similarly, use the positive strengths to make mantras and silently repeat them to yourself as you go about your day. Here are some examples of my mantras:

   - I am here to help others believe in who they are.
   - I am here to teach people to love who they are.
   - I want to be a nationally recognized motivational speaker to enlighten others on a grander scale.
   - I want to serve as a transition coach to help motivate and inspire people to embrace and love who they and become the best version of themselves.

3. On a regularly basis, list the ten things you love about yourself. It is not hard at all. Be honest with yourself. This "top ten" list should always be part of your life vision. Here is my top ten list of things I love about myself; these are the qualities that make me uniquely me:

   1. I am funny.
   2. I am kind.
   3. I am real.
   4. I am ambitious.
   5. I am VERY sensitive.
   6. I love.
   7. I am crazy, according to my son Ari!
   8. I am pretty.
   9. I am warm.
   10. I am open!

I know all the steps work. I have taken them myself and now, today, I am loving myself and my life. Okay, I know it took me several years, but that shows that it is possible to change at any age. If you want it badly enough, you will work through the pain and make it happen. I promise you, it's worth the effort.

Now then, just because you're done with the four steps to Bounce Back from a negative place in your life doesn't mean you're done with the work. Life will always happen. And, because it does, periodically you will find yourself in need of bouncing back again and again. These steps will always help you, but what will help the most is if you remain forever in love with yourself. To that end, start reading the next section and learn to have the greatest love affair of all.

Section 3
The Greatest
Love Affair
of All

Chapter Seven:
Lessons in Love

After two bad marriages and a bankruptcy, I was a shell of a person, simply going through life, and loving my children. I was desperate for someone to love me. I do not want to paint a picture that no one loved me. People did. My family, my friends, and I truly believe that my two ex-husbands did, too. I just didn't allow myself to feel it. I was too busy trying to make them love me.

I was willing to do anything to please people, thinking that if I did the "right" thing, then they would love me. I was the girl who would say *yes* to everyone, just so they would love me. I was constantly planning parties, saying *yes* to all invitations, all because I wanted people to like me and then maybe love me.

I did what I needed to do every day. I took care of the kids, paid bills, made sure my clients were happy. If my children and clients were happy and my bills were paid, then I thought that meant my life was good.

But I didn't feel loved. One day on the phone, I said to my dear friend Laura, "I don't know what it feels like to be loved."

She responded, very simply, "You need to let people in and let them show they care about you."

It sounded easy. But I had no idea how to do it.

Lesson number one: Love yourself

When I was forty-three years old my friend Susan said, "I want you to have the greatest love affair of all." I smiled and said, "I would like that but no one seems to want to fill the spot." She looked at me and said, "No, I want you to fall in love with you."

That is where my journey of self-love and my awakening really started. I remember the day I had called Laura, the day when I realized I never really felt loved. I also began to suspect that my expectations of what love is may have been a little off.

Through years of pain and personal growth, I began to realize that I was capable of not just being loved, but feeling loved, which is what I was seeking so desperately all along.

Please do not think that this was easy. I was hurt over and over because I wanted so badly to be loved and feel valued. I would idealize others to make them somehow appear more beautiful and special than they actually were. Everyone was always the prettier girl or the smarter girl, but now I know that I was and will always be just as pretty and smart as they are. It took years of work. Very hard work. That is the difference between buying a self-help book and actually making change: it takes work, lots and lots of work.

I decided to try what Susan told me to do. I pretended that I was going to romance someone else, but in reality, that someone was me. I decided it was time to have a love affair with myself.

So I made lists. First, I made a list of what I love to do. Then, I made a to-do list of things I wanted to do either alone or with someone.

Here is a list of a few things I enjoy doing just for me:

- Going out to the bookstore. I love to read a good book, but more importantly, I love to get lost in a bookstore. I started planning trips to read, relax, and take a journey through the aisles. Where do you love to go to get lost and to relax? Take yourself there.
- Having flowers everywhere. I've learned to treat myself as I would treat my best friend. We all tend to treat others better than we treat ourselves. Make a vow not to do that anymore. Pledge to make YOU the center of your world! Surround yourself with what you like to look at.
- Enjoying the taste of a delicious cold glass of wine or Diet Coke. How about a little bit of Sometimes I even say *screw the Diet! I'm going for regular, classic, old-fashioned Coca-Cola.* What's your favorite beverage? Coffee? Root beer? A latte or cappuccino? Take time to enjoy it, whatever it is, and savor it. Do not beat yourself up for taking time out of your day to do something so simple just for yourself. Taking a little time for self-indulgence and freedom will actually refresh you and give you the energy or spirit or whatever it is you might need to get through the rest of your day
- Thinking, reflecting, and being quiet. I am always thinking (sometimes it's not so positive), reflecting, and trying to be quiet. Quiet in the sense of being still with my thoughts and feelings. My therapist would say, *sit with your feelings, no matter what they are,*

which is not an easy task. Try it sometime: sit there and feel the unhappiness, the loneliness. Get to know it, and acknowledge it. We cannot overcome something negative in our lives or minds, if we don't even know it's there.

- Watching all things sports. Honestly one of my favorite things to do is watch sports and, on the odd occasion that I do it alone, it's a real treat. Sports are a part of my DNA. I cannot live without sports. I love to watch all the games, including football, baseball, basketball, and occasionally, I will play golf. (Okay, I admit it, I am not that good, but I do try.) Watching sports helps me to relax and breathe. Find what makes you feel the same way and be sure to schedule it in for yourself.

- Embracing my inner foodie. I love all types of food, so when I am alone, I make it *my* pick. I don't eat what my kids want and definitely not leftovers! Go to the market and buy the cheese you have wanted to try, or make the recipe you have wanted to take a stab at. Whatever you do, make it about you and you alone.

Lesson number two: Be your own best friend

One of the best ways to love yourself is to be your own best friend!

It's so easy to say, be your own best friend. Yet, we all find it so hard to do. It took me years of practice to learn and adapt this concept, and now, believe it or not, it comes perfectly natural to me.

What do I mean by being my own best friend? I mean, I treat myself the way I treat the people I love the most. After all, I love myself!

I love to surprise my friends and family with little things I know they will enjoy or that will simply make their day. When I pick up my younger son Ari from school, I will often have one of his favorite snacks on the seat waiting for him. It's easy, simple, and thoughtful to make him feel special. It's truly the little things.

So every once in a while, I treat myself to something I love such as my favorite candy bar or flowers, or just an hour of time to myself. I often hear myself saying to people: "You need to take some time." So I take my own advice. We all need time to think, process, and rejuvenate ourselves.

If we do not take time for ourselves, then we cannot make time and be there for others.

Another exercise I practice is self-talk. When I'm in a situation where I don't know quite what to do, I talk to myself as though I were talking to my best friend or someone I love. It's an exercise that takes work, practice, and patience but it's so worth it in the end.

Here's an example: Say you have a bad day at work. You could, like many of us, internalize the situation and beat yourself up about it as you drive home with a head full of negative self-talk. By the time you get home, your mood will only be worse and you wouldn't feel like taking the time to treat yourself right, like make a decent dinner, or allow yourself some downtime to relax and enjoy your family. Instead, you'd be more likely to stress eat and maybe even be snippy with your family. Your other option would be to talk to yourself like you would talk to your best friend. *So, you had a bad day? It's a just that, a bad day. It's done and over. Now the best thing to do is to learn from the experience. What could you have done differently? What could you do better next time? Remember when you handled something similar in the past with great results? You know you can do it again.* I believe everything in life is meant to teach us. We can use all our negative experiences as an opportunity to learn.

Lesson number three: Surround yourself with good people

Examine the people in your life the way your best friend would. Do you surround yourself with individuals who love and support you as your truest self?

When you want to make big changes in your life, when you want to get off the figurative treadmill of life because you're tired of running and running and not getting anywhere, you'll find it easier if you are surrounded by people who love you the way you should love yourself. So as you work through this book, take some time to look around and start rallying your troops. You might just need encouragement and support, but if you need help, all you have to do is ask.

There is no shame in asking a friend, family member, professor, or guidance counselor for help. Sometimes we all let our egos get in our way of getting the help we need or want. For some reason, we feel like we cannot and should not ask for help. Maybe we're worried people will think less of us for some reason. As human beings, we are governed by pride. But while pride is important, sometimes it makes us put on blinders, and then we don't see who's standing beside us. You're probably always willing to help a friend, so why wouldn't a friend want to do the same for you?

It's kind of funny that I started this section by using a treadmill for a metaphor because one of my greatest life lessons about friendship started on a treadmill.

I met one of my very best friends Wendy, who is truly like a sister to me, while running on a treadmill at the gym. I was running while she was on the stationary bike in front of me, and we started talking. We seemed to have an instant connection. Next thing you know, we were exchanging phone numbers and making plans to go out.

When we first became friends, Wendy shared her story about her divorce with me. I responded with, "No worries, I have been through this twice, it's a piece of cake! I will be by your side the entire time." In my mind, I was going to be the friend she needed at that time. The friend who understands the pain of divorce, the impact on the children, and the emotional rollercoaster. I lived up to my promise, and I was there for her. In this case, I served as something like a supportive teacher, and she as a student in need.

As time grew, so did our friendship, and she became the friend who never left my side, too.

Wendy, who is one of the nicest, sweetest human beings I know, was in a bad car accident and faced with life-threatening injuries. She fought hard to come back and make a full recovery. Her mantra in life is to "live for today," words that stuck with me.

Live for today? I would fight it in my head because I am such a serious type-A personality. I could not wrap my head around not planning for a plan B, or a "what if?" But Wendy insisted: "Lisa, you have to live for today." With this mantra, Wendy became my teacher, and has helped me instill this philosophy in my everyday living and learning. Through good times and bad. Heartaches and joys.

I am sharing this story because you never know who will enter your life, when they will enter, or why. To me, that is one of the most beautiful things about life. I thought I was put into Wendy's life to help, love, and support her through her divorce. Wendy has taught me so much, and she continues to amaze me with her strength, compassion, and kindness. We all need a Wendy in our life. I wonder how different my life would have been if I hadn't gone to the gym that day, been on that treadmill, and looked up to see her beautiful face. Or what if neither of us were willing to let go of our pride? We never would have been able to help each other.

The truth is that Wendy was in pain, and I was, too. We both needed to rally our troops for love and support through our difficult journeys ahead of us.

Self-love Exercises

1. The selfie exercise: Take a picture of yourself, every day, and really take the time to examine and familiarize yourself with your own unique characteristics and physical attributes. Then take the "selfie" exercise one

step further. Write down and make note of what you love most about yourself. Is it your smile? A twinkle in your eyes? Maybe a perfectly placed set of dimples! In these unique traits, you will find the traces of your inner energy, the goodness at your core that makes you *you*, inside and out. Look for that unique beauty, and then share it with others!

Point out to your friends what you love about yourself, and then ask them to do the same with their own selfies. This is not about being conceited; it's about celebrating ourselves and those we love for exactly who we are.

2. It's a me kinda day! Take yourself out for the day, design a day just for you. We do it all the time for our friends, right? We plan a girls' day or night out. Why not do it just for you? My idea of a perfect me day always starts at the gym, then maybe lunch with a friend, nails, shopping and then whatever I want. Yes, whatever I want.

3. Write a list of nice things you have done in the past for your friends. Review the list, then ask *what have you done for yourself lately?*

4. Gift time! Buy yourself something that you want. A necklace or a bracelet, perfume, whatever.

5. Kindness! Always remember to be kind to yourself just like you would be to your friends. Speak with kindness. Show kindness.

This final exercise is so important, I felt the need to separate it and put it here all by itself: don't *ever* forget to celebrate your birthday!

Everyone who knows me knows that I love, love, love birthdays! Why? Because that is the one day that truly belongs to me. Yes, me. I get to celebrate me, and my friends and family take the time to really celebrate me! Through the years, my friends and colleagues have laughed and always told me, "Lisa, you celebrate your birthday for a month!" In my house and to my kids, our birthdays entail "birthday weeks."

While I do think every day should be celebrated and embraced, your birthday is the one day you can make all about YOU! Celebrate *you* coming into this world.

Chapter 8:
Making Choices

I truly believe life is one continual choice after another. If you want to feel good about yourself, you have to make choices that allow you to do so. You have to choose to engage in behaviors that make you feel good.

My aunt once told me that life is living the choices you make.

I remember always wanting my aunt's life. Yes, I know, we are not supposed to want someone else's life. What I guess I really wanted was to love myself the way she loves herself. When it comes to being happy and content in life, she has it covered. I admire my aunt for so many reasons. She is a great example of someone who never lets the world get the best of her. She keeps moving forward, creating the life she wants and believes in. While raising two kids, she went back to school as an adult to become a special education teacher. She and my Uncle T (short for Ted) were always the couple I admired. They raised two great kids, my cousins Jodie and Joel. Jodie is like a sister to me. She's everything I thought I wanted to be growing up: pretty, thin, and the "popular girl." Thankfully, I never allowed my own insecurity to get in the way of loving her and her children. I feel nothing but adoration and love toward my aunt and uncle, cousins, and their families.

Having a relationship like the one I have with my family is my choice. I choose to love them unconditionally, and knowing they love me back is priceless to me. Because, finally, I can feel and believe that I am loved.

Think about how you approach life. Realize whether you love yourself or not is a choice.

Choosing to be Happy

When you start your day, do you decide to be happy? Do you see the glass half full or half empty? It has so much to do with how we look at the glass. We really do make matters or obstacles in our life harder than they are, and we do not have to.

Today, I was in a meeting, and a woman said to me, "Lisa, you always have such positive energy." It's not the first time someone said something like that to me. I mean, my nickname as always been "Sunshine." However, I don't always wake up all "Suzy-Sunshine" and glowing. But, and this is a big BUT, a major part of my philosophy is to wake up and think about my thoughts.

No, that was not a typo, so I'll repeat it: I think about my thoughts. If I begin to doubt myself or believe that something won't work, or when negative thoughts try to take over, I fight back in my head. I challenge those thoughts, my own thoughts, with new ones. It may sound crazy, but it's really quite simple. It's just a more interactive and challenging form of self-talk. We all have the power to talk to ourselves. You just have to decide if and when you are ready to listen to the good and the bad, and to challenge yourself when your thoughts need challenging or a new perspective.

Some of us, myself in particular, think we are not deserving of all the good we have. But we are. We really are. Every one of us is. We only have one life to live, and we need to stop convincing ourselves that living in drama or fear or unhappiness is the only way to become worthy of the good we have. Think about it: fear and unhappiness are emotions. They are states of being that we have power over.

Every day I wake up and say, choose to say, "I am the luckiest woman in the world." And I believe it! I have two wonderful healthy boys, family and friends whom I love and adore, and the best career, with an added bonus of being lucky enough to teach.

Other than being a mom, there is nothing as rewarding to me as being a teacher. Becoming an adjunct professor was one of the best decisions I have ever made, and the experience has helped shape the new "bounce back" version of myself over the past few years. I wish I could personally thank all of my students for what they have taught me. Some students have taught me patience and kindness. Some have taught me how to slow down, rethink how I am presenting an idea, or simply how to be flexible.

When I was a student teacher, the lead teacher would always say to me, "Teaching is like life: You must be flexible. You cannot rush through a chapter simply because your planner says you have to be done. You have to make sure your students are learning and grasping the material."

Throughout my teaching experience, I have challenged my students to think big, to reach for the stars, and most importantly to believe in themselves. And although most have probably never realized it, they have helped me to do the same.

We all have the ability to have a wonderful life. Notice I did not say perfect.

I said wonderful; whatever wonderful means for you! Believe in who you are, and remember to make every day a special day. Find something wonderful about the day, even if it's reading and learning something new on the Internet. It can be that simple. Some of the best things in life are the simple things, and more often than not, they are free.

Yes, happiness is a state of mind that you choose to take. And I choose to see the positive in others and in life.

Here are some more exercises I do when I want to choose to feel happy but am in a difficult situation:

1. I have a gratitude journal where I list everything I am appreciative of.
2. I smile when I don't feel like smiling.
3. I create a mantra about living a happy life, and embrace it.
4. I write a list of what makes me really happy.
5. I think about activities that make me feel alive and happy, then make plans to do them as soon as possible to give myself something wonderful to look forward to.

Here's my list:

- **Being with Jacob and Ari. We could be doing nothing at all. Some of our greatest memories are of when we were simply doing nothing but spending time together.**
- **Teaching. I love being with my students. Motivating anyone to learn and be the best they can be makes me feel pure joy.**
- **Hugs. I love to hug my children and basically all my friends, family, and yes, my clients! There is no replacement for a good hug.**
- **Holiday dinners. To me, there is nothing better than filling my home with friends and family to celebrate a holiday. It's never about the food. It's always about the love and friendship in the room.**
- **Parades. I absolutely love parades such as the Thanksgiving Day Parade, the Mummers Parade (a Philadelphia tradition). If there is a parade, I am one very happy girl.**

Choosing to Find the Good

When I was growing up in Northeast Philly, one of my closest friends Pam

67

lived right around the corner from me, and we were always ready to go out. We would call each other and say, "Are you ready to go out?" Next thing you knew, she was honking the horn in front of my house. I would run out the door and then off we'd go in her Chevy Camaro (which, unsurprisingly, we thought was the coolest car ever).

Pam and I worked together, traveled together; essentially, we grew up together. Pam was always supportive of me, no matter what I did. I tried stand-up comedy for a few years, and Pam never missed a show. She was always there and laughing, and she continues to be there. Having lifelong friends is a true gift.

Both of Pam's parents died very suddenly. I was by her mother's side with her entire family when she died, which was an honor. Dolores was a gift to anyone who knew her. Not only did she love her daughters, she loved their friends too. Her funeral was one the most uplifting I have ever attended.

It could have been depressing and overwhelmingly sad, but people were sharing wonderful stories about her, and laughter filled the room. We all made the choice to focus on Delores' beautiful legacy. We paid tribute to her and how she lived her life. She was loving, accepting, warm, and very kind and funny. We all know you need a sense of humor to get through this journey. But kindness is key, and Dolores was never afraid to share her kind heart. Her death reminded me of some of the greater messages and meaning in life. As I walked out of the funeral home, I promised myself that when I die I will leave a legacy, too, of making people feel loved and reminding them how they are special.

Realizing that Dolores' loving nature was what we would always remember about her is what helped us all heal from her passing, and taught me a huge lesson in life. Pam's mom taught me that people will always remember how you make them feel. And if you feel good about yourself, you can make people feel good about who they are, too. So why not make that critical choice and love yourself now? You will be in good service to everyone you meet.

Remember, we all have the same opportunity for happiness. It's a choice.

Remember you have to take care of YOU before you can take care of anyone else.

Ongoing Choices

My love affair with myself continues every day, because I choose to continue it. I wake up each morning and make sure I'm intent on having a fabulous day because I deserve it. I begin by asking, "Who am I going to meet? What exciting thing is going to happen?" Then my daily mantra is as follows: "If I don't take care of me, then nothing else can fall into place."

It is not selfish to love yourself, it is necessary. You cannot reach your goals, you cannot be the kind of parent/spouse/friend/anything that you want to be unless you find yourself worthy of being so. And the path to worthiness starts with finding yourself lovable.

In Step One of my Bounce Back Into You plan, you learned what kinds of beliefs you're engaging in that are preventing you from being happy. But if you don't love and honor yourself, you'll never be able to change those beliefs.

In Step Two, you got real and took responsibility for your role in your situations and relationships. But, if you don't love yourself, then you'll put yourself right back into those negative situations because you won't feel worthy enough to do otherwise.

In Step Three, you created a vision of what you want your life to be like. But you can only imagine a good life if you love yourself enough to believe your worth receiving it.

And finally, as we learned in Step Four, you'll have difficulty creating any kind of lasting change in your life if you don't create the change in yourself first by loving yourself.

Only when you love yourself unconditionally will you be confident enough to fully express yourself and to fully engage in life with certainty and strength.

Learning to love yourself is how you can find the greatness and beauty that's within you. Not only that but, it's how you'll recognize the potential for more that's within you.

No matter what, life happens. As I've expressed in this book already, the key to being able to bounce back when life happens is to love yourself—you love you.

Section 4
Maintaining
your
Bounce

Chapter 9:
When Life Continues to Happen

Even after you complete the four steps, life will continue to happen and present new opportunities to bounce back. Repeating the four steps will help, but what will give you the strength to do it and make lasting change will be to thoroughly love yourself. In other words, you gotta do both!

Weathering Storms

Weathering a bad storm will also be easier if you continue to love yourself as you go through it. One thing I like to do is I make sure I always have easy access to things that make me smile. Here are a few examples:

1. I created an "I Love Lisa" board in my office. It's a bulletin board filled with things that make me smile, like my son's high school graduation program book where his name is listed as one of the students who earned straight A's all four years of high school. There are handwritten notes from my younger son who is always telling me how much he loves me and why. There are countless thank-you notes from my students. This board is designed to make me, and only me, feel good about myself, my work, and my life, and it serves as a constant reminder of how I touch people's lives.

2. I also love surrounding myself with things that remind me of how blessed I am, so I have pictures of my boys all over the house, my office, living room, family room, and bedroom. I never get tired of looking at them; they are my heart. One of my favorite things to do is save their artwork from school. I treasure everything they have made for me, from the handprints to the first love note.

3. I also have a "Feel Good Book." It's a regular notebook filled with nice things that I want to remember, from a special day I shared with a friend to a moment that made me smile. I started writing in it years ago, and it serves as my book when I need a personal pick-me-up.

4. Some days we all need a reminder of how special we are. If there is one thing I have learned, though, it's that I have to take personal responsibility for my own happiness. I used to rely on others to validate me and make me feel good. Today, after years of bouncing back and working on my mind and spirit every day, I know I am the only one who can validate me.

5. Be creative and find a way to have fun with the storm. My younger son, Ari, is not a big fan of Mondays. Okay, who really loves Mondays, right? So we created Magical Monday. Now, every Monday after school we do something *he* wants to do. Sometimes we go to the park and ride bikes, sometimes we have ice cream for dinner, or sometimes we just hang out and watch Monday Night Football. We created Magical Monday to make Monday morning more palatable for Ari. We also have Wacky Wednesday because we were having so much fun with our Mondays. Anything goes on Wacky Wednesday for dinner and then we have after-dinner fun activity.

Here are a few more exercises that will make you feel good when times are tough:

- Spread the Love. If you haven't told someone lately how much you love them, write a letter today or an e-mail. It feels great to tell people you love and appreciate them. For me, appreciation is one of the greatest gifts we can give.
- Create a Love Box. Make a love box. Take an old shoe box and decorate it anyway you want. Fill it with pictures of you and the people you love, or a shell from the beach, anything that will remind you of how loved you are and how wonderful your life is!
- Make a Sticky Note Reminder. This is one of my favorite things to do. When I am trying to do something like go to the gym on a regular basis, I will write myself notes that say, "Take care of you, or no one else will." Write yourself reminders to take care of YOU!
- Create a Happiness Journal, and every day write down what YOU DID to make yourself happy each day!

As you may have noticed, I like to make lists and write things down. So you probably won't be surprised to learn that when life happens to me, another practice I have in place is to write down whatever I am feeling. Try it. Just write it down and then walk away from the problem. Or, as I like to say, "Put it in a box on a shelf until you are ready to deal with it."

Try to wait until the emotion is not so high, and then you can go back and read the notes. You will probably then make a decision based on facts rather than feelings. You'll also discover that writing down *why* you're upset helps to clear your head about the subject.

Believe it or not, my oldest son Jacob was the one to teach me this practice. Jacob is a mature young man who has the ability to listen, process, and then discuss his thoughts based on logic, not emotion. He's the opposite of me. I'm probably one of the most emotional human beings around. The good news is that is what makes me *me*. But once I started writing through the situations, I was able to make myself think more logically and rationally.

I also write before I have difficult discussions or conversations with family, friends, coworkers, and so on. It was so hard for me to do that because I was very afraid of being wrong, or that the person would not like me or not want to work with me anymore.

I learned to write letters to the person with whom I wished to communicate. I would write a letter about the situation, almost do a situational analysis of what was working and what wasn't, and how I could make it better. Then, I'd put it away and decide later, when I was not so emotional, if I understand my role in the situation. Or I determine that the conversation is no longer necessary because I have worked it out by myself and now I feel at peace with it.

My recommendation is to write the letter to help you understand the situation. If you write a letter to someone when you are happy or upset, you can often discover and understand the *why* behind your emotions. Writing the letter makes you gain clarity on the situation. By the way, I am suggesting you write the letter for your eyes only. This exercise is for *you* to get clarity.

When the emotion isn't so high, read the letter. Look for YOU in it. Recognize the parts of the letter that were written in an emotional moment, and the parts of the issue that still resonate as true and valid to you now that you had a chance to get some time and distance from the situation. Can you look in your past and see a pattern with this issue in this letter? What about this person or issue is yours? What do you really have control over in the situation? What is not in your power to change?

The letter writing exercises are freeing, and here's why: YOU can change what you do not like about yourself! You have the power. Once you begin to recognize what you don't like, you can begin the work needed to make it better! Try them and see if you can spot what issues, feelings, sentiments, or associations in YOU are causing or affecting what's bothering you about the coworker, friend, family member, and so on. This is about taking care of you; you're giving yourself the opportunity to gain clarity in situations. You're giving yourself a way to attain an internal sense of peace.

I know we do not always have the time to stop and write a letter. So I suggest this "expedited" version of that practice: Ask the questions in your head. Then, look inside YOU for the answers. And be honest with yourself, you know, like how your best friend would be honest with you. (PS: When you're calm, don't forget to write a love letter to yourself to serve as a reminder of how beautiful you are inside and out.)

More on the Power of Words

Sometimes the storms we weather because life happens have nothing to do with us, we just think they do. What do I mean? I'm talking about the way people use words that makes us feel less than, unworthy, unlovable, and so on. We must learn to separate someone's words from how we feel about ourselves. Let me explain by telling you about my grandfather.

I am not sure exactly how old I was, but I can still recall this one moment like it was yesterday. My grandfather, known to us grandkids as Poppy, looked at my one cousin, who was always the prettiest, and said to her, "You are so pretty." He never said anything like that to me, even in that moment, when I sat right beside him and my cousin.

It wasn't what he said; it was what he didn't say. For me, it was as if he was silently saying to me, "You are not pretty," and in my head I interpreted that as, "You are not good enough." We all do this. We interpret what we think we heard. We write and create scripts in our head, and then we do not take the time to revisit those thoughts and inflated scenarios we created. We all have people in our life that for some reason tease us or make remarks that are not meant to hurt us, but they do. Why is that?

Is it genuine teasing to be funny, or playful? Or is it jealousy?

For years I would care to the point of obsession, and ask myself repeatedly, "Why did they say that? What did they mean by that?" As I have grown more confident in my ability to be myself, I have reached a point in my life where I just don't, and can't, care anymore about what others think. It took time for me to get there. I promise you that you will get there, too. And you will find, it doesn't serve you to care what others think.

I don't ask myself any questions like that anymore. Instead, I talk to myself, or repeat mantras, such as: *I am me, and this works for me.* When someone makes a comment directed to you, who you are, or how you live your life, try talking to yourself rather than obsessing about their comment. That person cannot change the truth, no matter what he or she says. You are you, and it's your life.

I have endured many comments that were directed to me with the intent to hurt or shake, and in the past, they did hurt me. When you have bad self-esteem and someone says something about you in a negative way, it can impact you severely. At the early age of eighteen, my hair started to turn gray, and I chose to dye it red. I picked red as my hair color because my grandmother had red hair and so did Lucille Ball. Those were two women I loved, admired, and who could always make me laugh. Some people have been bold enough to tell me, to my face, that my hair color is not real. To which I say, "Well, too bad. I like it, and it stays."

It's my life, and I get to choose.

What I have learned through the years is that we have no control over what others say to us. What we can control is our reaction to their words. We all have the ability to control the conversation in our heads. Yes, in our heads. Talk to yourself with love, kindness, and forgiveness. We all need to be kinder to ourselves, because the rest of the world isn't going to be. Remind yourself, over and over again of the following: it's your life and you have to be true to who you are. No one else knows better than you do what you need, what you like, what is right for you. So there's not need to value someone else's opinions of you over your own opinions of yourself.

Words are so very powerful. In one conversation and exchange of words, feelings, egos, and morale can be damaged. You never really know the impact one conversation can have on you or the other person. I try to stop myself from my first response to avoid saying things that will have a lasting impact and are unnecessarily hurtful, particularly in a heated or tense conversation.

One day I was driving with a former friend of mine, and we were talking about my pending divorce from my second husband. We were discussing the value and importance of therapy and how people are willing to spend money on their clothes, hair, makeup, gym memberships, and the like, but often are not willing to spend money on their minds. I mentioned that another friend of mine had recommended a really good therapist, and I was considering going to see him. Her response was, "You are cooked. You have seen other therapists before. Just focus on your children, and get them therapy. You are basically baked, and people do not change."

All I can say is, *thank God* I did not listen to her. She was totally wrong. People do change when they want to work hard, and are open to change. If I had listened to her, I would still be stuck where I was. I knew after my second marriage failed, I needed to change.

Remember that story.

People, friends, and family will offer their best advice. Please do not eat, sleep, and live by their opinions, that's what their advice is, you know. Remember, they are offering this advice from the places they are coming from, from *their* own experience. It's not your place, it's theirs! You can change if you want to, and you don't have to do it their way.

> **If you think you need advice, ask for it! Seek it out. There are self-help books, life coaches, motivational speakers, online webinars, and a ton of online "feel-good" voices everywhere. Keep searching until you can feel in your gut that you got the answers you needed. And, if you cannot find it in those places, do find a therapist in your community. Do not make an excuse and say, "I cannot afford one," because there are plenty of free social service programs.**
>
> **For me, therapy was a turning point in my life. My therapist, Dr. Michael Plumeri, is more than just my therapist. He is instrumental in my life as he constantly opens up my mind to the possibilities of my own continual growth. Without him, I am fairly certain I would not be writing this book. For that matter, if he and I did not work as hard as we did, I am not sure I would be as happy as I am today. Because, I know you have heard me say this before, it takes work.**
>
> **Dr. P, as I like to call him, always says to me, "It's the work you do after the forty-five minute session that makes a difference. Some people are just not willing to do the work.**

Every time I think about my former friend saying that I was cooked, I remind myself about two things:

1. No one, I repeat, no one, is all-knowing, even though some people do leave us with the impression that they are. I used to look to others for the answer. Then I realized that there is no such thing as "the answer" or "the secret." You can gain wisdom from some people, sure. But, you have to get in tune with who you are, what you value, and what you want from life before

their wisdom can actually help or, even better, before your own wisdom tells you what to do. You have to be willing to take the steps that will lead you to the answers that can work for *you* and your happiness.

2. I remind myself that being self-righteous sucks. My former friend was very self-righteous with her response. When my friends or family ask for my advice, I always preface it by saying, "This works for me," or "This is how I interpret the situation," because truly in the end, no one has all the answers for you. Only you can know your truth once you fall in love with who you are. You will realize that there is no greater journey to go on than to find self-love, no matter what anyone else tells you.

Next time someone says something to you: STOP, THINK, and ASK YOURSELF the following:

*   Why are they saying this?
*   Who are they?
*   Do they matter?
*   Do I respect their opinion?

When my former friend made that self-righteous statement, I called my dear friend Lynda who is a key team member of mine. Here's what Lynda asked me about my former friend: "Does she really matter? What role does she play in your life? Seriously, does she matter?"

When I am faced with adversity, I take time to pause, process, and ponder what I can and should do. I always try to pretend I am the other person and think about who, what, and why? Who are they? What are they really upset about or saying? Why did they say it?

But don't think I'm only talking about the words other people use. We *all* need to spend more time watching our words and actions. They are our greatest instruments of power. People might not remember your exact words, but the impact might have a lasting effect.

When life happens and we find we're weathering a storm based on what someone says, we all need to take the time to stop, breathe, and remind ourselves: *Words have the power to inspire or destroy. They can bring a dream to life or kill it forever.*

Chapter 10:
Perspective and Balance

I was just talking about getting perspective when it comes to what other people say to us. And really, I think life is all about perspective. It is about how we decide, how we choose, to look at something, to perceive it. Meaning, if you are looking out your living-room window, and it's rainy and dreary, it can make you feel sad or lonely, or any emotion evoked by the darkness and bleakness. But we don't have to feel that way. We can be appreciative of how nighttime gives us a chance to rest and heal. We can be grateful for those dreary days because they mean either we had rain or will get some soon and the plants need water.

Perspective

We all look through two sets of personal windows. One set is our eyes that we use to see the physical world. The other set is our perspective to interpret that world and tell us what it means to us. We all have our window to look through and just because it was dark at one time, does not mean it has to stay that way. How you look at life, your perspective, is your decision. Your choices are how you gain perspective on all situations.

I will never forget the first time my mom told me that she thought I'd had a hard life. She said, "Lisa, I am not sure why, but you seem to have had a hard life."

I remember that moment vividly and precisely, and how I thought about it and thought about it, over and over. It really bothered me because honestly, in my mind I didn't think my life was so hard. To me, I had a few bumps in the road, but doesn't everyone?

It's almost funny to think about it. I felt unattractive, too tall, bird-nesty, not smart enough, unloved, and unworthy for most of my life, but by the time my mother asked me that question because I was in a good place in my life, none of it seemed that bad. I was able to think clearer on it and put it all into perspective. Compared to some people in the world, I had a great life, so who was I to complain?

Then I started to think about it more and more, and I started to listen, watch, and observe more. Because I wanted to know: Did I have a hard life? Was my life harder than others? I started to ask the question to my friends, "Do you think your life is hard?" I was surprised by the variety of answers. The overall conclusion was that life is not meant to be easy. Okay, let me say that again. Life is not meant to be easy. No one ever said that life was intended to be easy; however, among my friends' answers, there was a common theme. That is, perspective played an overriding factor in determining whether they viewed life as easy or hard.

It took some time to understand what my mom was saying. Basically, she was saying that in her opinion and from her perspective, my life was hard. She was looking at my life from her vantage point, or as I like to say, from her window. It made me realize that when people say things to me or to you, it's important to remember that those words and opinions are from their perspective and experience. It's not good or bad. It's just theirs. And the good news is that you get to decide what you see and how you perceive your world when you look out your window.

Once I determine what window someone is looking out of, I can understand why someone said what they did.

I also believe that as a mom, my mother wanted me to live a life with a happy marriage and to not have to work as hard as I do. And that is okay because as a mom or friend, we all want what we think will make the person happy. I don't think she realizes I love what I do for a living. From her window, I work too hard, and I'm twice divorced; therefore, my life is hard. From my window, everything I went through was supposed to happen, and even though it hasn't been easy all of the time, it certainly hasn't been hard.

If I hadn't experienced the events and trials in my life, I would not be where I am today: writing this book to help remind you that it's your life, and your choice. It's your story. You are the writer of your script. You are the producer, director, and principal actor in your life's movie. You are the lead, so never forget to give yourself top billing. And try to remember that as you watch other people's movies, you are watching it through your window, and you will never find someone that looks out the same exact window as you. That's okay. Remember you have the option to be part of other people's movies. It's your choice. You get to choose what movies you want to be in and what roles you want to play.

The same can be said for your emotional state. It's a matter of perspective.

Are you a happy person?

What do you see when you look out of your lenses, your eyes? I see happiness.

Gain Perspective Exercise

One way to honestly assess where your perspective is on yourself, is to think about yourself the way you think about others. For example, we all have that one friend who complains endlessly about something insignificant. He or she never lets it go and has earned the title of "the complainer." Then there is the "woe is me, my life stinks" friend. He or she wants your sympathy but will never really do anything to change the situation. This type of friend presents him or herself as "the victim."

Think on your patterns of thoughts and behaviors and see what label you can come up with for yourself.

Ask:

- Who are you now?
- Do you find yourself complaining all the time but seldom, if ever, finding solutions? Are you the complainer?
- Do you think that people always disrespect you? Or that they are always getting what they want at your expense? Are you the victim?
- Do you feel like you're the one who always has to do it all, that nothing gets done (or done right) unless you do it, so you're tired, sore, whatever? Are you the martyr?
- Or do you find solutions? Do you see the good in others? Are you the optimist?

Keep thinking about the kinds of people in your life and how you describe them, as you do so, keep coming up with questions to ask yourself until you think you've found the right term to describe yourself.

Now then, when you get a clear view of yourself, a clear perspective, ask: *is that who I want to be?*

I remember at a very young age, I was told I look through the world with rose-colored glasses. I didn't really understand what that meant. But now, as I approach fifty, and with many valuable experiences and lessons behind me, I can honestly say that I would rather look through beautiful, rose-colored glasses than colorless or dark ones. It's a choice. Your perspective is a choice.

Balance

After you gain perspective on who you are and what your life is really like, then you can begin to address what you need and who you want in your life to find balance. Sometimes that means purging. Though I find it somewhat comical when my forty-something friends say, "I had to purge so-and-so."

I laugh because it's like an announcement. They are so proud of the fact that they no longer want to be friends with someone. They say it like it's an awakening.

Well, I am here to say we should all have our own personal awakening on an ongoing basis. Why not? Why not take the time to do a personal inventory on who has a place in your life? Who has a different place in your life than where he/she stood before? Or, who no longer fits at all?

Remember, it's your life, and you have the right to decide how you live your life and with whom.

A good cleanse is all the rage in the fitness and wellness world, so why not do a good cleanse for you and your life? Yes, you deserve a fresh start—or as I like to say: *a time to reboot!*

When you do a cleanse, you usually do not eat for a few days, or you eat a certain fruit or vegetable for a few days. Cleanse and balance: the perfect combination.

When I need a cleanse and balance, I like to create alone time. I make sure I take time, even if only for ten minutes, to get in touch with myself. I create those moments of absolute stillness, physical and mental–like a fast from food, only it's a fast from stimulation–to reflect and listen to what my gut is really saying. It gives me a chance to sort out all the mixed messages in my body and mind and to do a personal inventory to help me discern what's really going on in my relationships.

> I love, love, love my alone time. In today's busy world with all of us staying so connected, I highly recommend you take time for you and you alone. But because sometimes my busy days get away from me, one of my favorite things to do is to lie in bed in the morning, before anyone else is up, and have a positive conversation with myself so that I make sure I get at least a little bit of quality time alone every day. It starts out with an affirmation for the day. I try to create a new one every day. They are so simple, like "Today, you will smile all day at everyone, and you will make someone's day." I generally love to smile, so smiling comes naturally to me, and I believe that it is good for the soul.

That quiet time is also a good time to balance out who you think you are with how other people view you. That is, you get a chance to determine if the persona you're projecting to the world. Does it match you, for real?

People who know me, know that I often ask the following question of a friend or family member when their relationships are being tested on compassion and empathy: "At the core, is he or she a good person?" You can apply that same question to yourself. Do a reality check and listen to your gut as you continue asking the tough questions: "Am I a good person? Did I handle that situation with compassion? Could I have done better? Did I do my best to articulate my thoughts so the person I was talking to understood my point of view?" And here is my favorite, "Did I try to put myself in the other's place and consider how he or she was feeling?"

Answer these questions honestly. Self-reflection and evaluation is crucial to growth and moving forward. If you cannot ask the tough questions and answer them honestly, then how can you grow?

I continue to be a reflective person and do my daily exercises to stay on my path of growth and evolution. I will continue to ask myself these questions and more, such as, "Am I making a contribution? Am I making a difference? If I am not making a contribution to my family and friends, then what is standing in my way?"

I believe we are here to contribute. We are all here for a common good: to be good people and bring out the best in others. My personal growth is an essential part of living for me, not unlike how eating is essential to my survival. I am always doing a reality check to gain perspective and achieve balance in my life.

Remember, we all go through trying times in our lives, but that does not define who we are as people. We define who we are, therefore we decide whether or not we are happy with our lives. And, if we are not happy, then we are the ones who can change ourselves and learn to love ourselves.

One more note on balance: balance isn't just a matter of being surrounded by the right people and making sure you have alone time to figure out what's really going on in your relationships. It's also a matter of managing the amount of energy you're putting out into the world.

Energy balance has always been hard for me. I used to live my life all or nothing, but eventually I became exhausted. Over time, I have learned the importance of balance. And now I think we all need to create our own sense of balance, and accept that what works for one might not work for another. I have friends who I would call "workaholics," but they balance working hard during the week with playing hard on the weekend because that's what works for them. There really is not an ideal definition of balance for everyone. It's up to you and you alone to create your sense of balance and harmony.

The one thing I want you to remember and hold onto is that who you are today is not who you will be tomorrow. If you decide to change, you will! If you decide to live your life for you and only you, you will succeed in your journey toward self-love, and you will see your missteps as opportunities for growth. That's a matter of perspective. Taking the time to think about why the missteps happened so that you can prevent them in the future, means you're finding balance in your life. You're not running on that treadmill all the time. You're stepping off to get create a change

.

Chapter 11:
A Magical Life

We are all unique individuals, like snowflakes. And I think snowflakes make the world seem magical. Snow, in its brilliant sparkle, blankets the world around us (or at least the Northeast coast) and changes the landscape from ordinary to extraordinary. I always enjoy sitting quietly and watching the snow fall as I reflect and remember that we, each and every one of us, are like snowflakes. Each has its own shape, size, and uniqueness. But together we can make something magical.

My boys are my magic. One day, they will have their own wives and children, and will continue to make magic, build their lives, and create love. My hope for them is that they live their lives filled with self-love, acceptance, and magic; their own version of magic, not mine. As a parent, I think it's our job to help our children believe in themselves, and set them on the right path to creating a magical existence.

As a child, my parents were not perfect. Growing up, I so badly wanted them to be perfect, to say the right thing, and do the right thing. Today, I realize there is no such thing as doing or saying the right thing, and that I placed unrealistic expectations on them. They might not have been perfect the way I wanted them to be, but they were their own version of perfect.

What's amazing to me, or should I say refreshing, is that the more I love, accept, and believe in myself, the more I love my family. Why? Because that's just the way it works. When you learn to love yourself unconditionally, you automatically learn to do the same with the people around you. Maybe it's because you learn to dedicate yourself to being happy, which means you let go of old grievances and realize we're all doing the best we can. When you focus on that, it's easy to love your family and friends for who they are and not for who you wished and hoped they would be.

My mom taught me how to be strong, independent, and most of all, how to be a great mom. She led by example, and today, I can see that she taught me how to never give up, always work hard, and love my children like no one else can. I adore my mom for the woman she is. I don't look back anymore and say, "I wish she did this" or "I wish she was more like so-and-so's mom." I am who I am because my mom never gave up on me, ever. My mom is my advocate and cheerleader, something that I will always be for my children.

I mentioned earlier that my dad was a gutsy man, gutsy and wonderful! I applaud my dad for marrying my mom with three young children. There were not a lot of men back then (nor today) who would marry a woman with so much responsibility and history, and then raise those children like their own.

My brothers, Michael and Larry, and I are not as close as I would like to be. We are friendly, and we love each other, but we are not geographically or emotionally close. They have their lives, and I have mine, and that's okay.

My aunt and uncle continue to play a major role in my life. Through the years, they were my second set of parents. Today, they are my friends whom I adore and admire.

When I set out to write this book, it was and continues to be an opportunity to share my experiences and help others learn from my past, present, and future. My goal is to tell you and convince you that you are not alone!

You have read that my childhood was riddled with insecurity and self-doubt. As I grew up, my life's journey was filled with quiet heartache, pain, and struggle.

Yet, today, I continue to have the greatest love affair with myself. I have been an adjunct professor for almost ten years. And I have been working on hosting a TV show called Bouncing Back with Lisa Bien. The goal of the show is to talk about self-love and acceptance, and to openly discuss personal adversities in life and how we must all bounce back.

For the first time in my life, I am coproducing a TV show and serving as the host. It is not an easy task. I love the mission of the show, but I have to be honest, it is pushing me way out of my comfort zone. The head producer of the show is Paul. He has more than thirty-eight years of experience in the television business. Paul is patient and has served as my teacher throughout this process. Every time I leave a shoot, I feel drained. I find myself going back into old habits, thinking to myself, "Oh my God, I am not good enough to take on a project like this." But the truth of the matter is that I am good enough. I am simply learning new skills. I am now the student. Being a student does not just entail sitting at a desk and learning, in the formal sense of the word. It also means learning from someone with more experience and esteem in a certain area than you, someone who is willing to work with you, advise and guide you, and encourage your growth. Even if that means a little tough love.

As you go through life, ask yourself who in your relationships is the teacher, and who is the student? What lessons are available for me to learn here? How can I grow?

Personal growth is the work I have been talking about throughout this book. It means taking the steps to work on YOU. It means you are open to being the student. I have to remind myself that being a student is just as important as being a teacher. Some days, these lessons are just good reminders that we are all here to grow.

For me, going on a journey to find self-love and acceptance was a necessity, not an option. I went on this journey to learn how to love myself unconditionally. Along the way I found that not only could I love myself so entirely, I could also love many others. Now that I have discovered self-love and acceptance, I am more than capable of loving others exactly the way they are. There's no more wishing they would say or do things differently.

Today, and for the rest of my life, I will embrace love of myself, my family, and friends. The ongoing theme throughout this book is that in the end, it's all about love, self-love first, and then love for others. My philosophy about life is that we are only here once, and we should learn to love ourselves no matter what life throws our way.

We will be tested, and life is not always going to be easy, but if we love ourselves enough and allow others to love us, the journey will be much better and sweeter.

It took me years to feel and embrace love. What taught me unconditional love was the birth of my first son Jacob. He completely and entirely changed my life. I remember the day he was born. The nurse brought him into the room, and he was the most beautiful baby. I held him and looked at him, touched his little fingers, and was in total awe of him and the gift of life. It was truly magical. I remember saying to him: "Jacob, I have never been a mom before, but I promise to do my best, to always love you, no matter what, and together we can figure this out." It was Jacob who taught me what unconditional love feels like. As a mom you learn to love no matter what, and then you can accept the love in return.

Years later, my life was blessed with my sweet, sweet Ari. I am sure most parents can relate to this: when you have a second child you question your ability to love another child as much or the same. We all question that. Ari and I have a loving mother-son relationship that is nothing less than magical. His passion and love of life are a constant reminder to me of how blessed I am because I have two wonderful sons. They are both loving and passionate boys with very, very bright futures.

Being a mom has taught me what love looks like. All I have to do to remind myself of the meaning of love is to look at a picture of my children, or even just think about them.

Life is not meant to be lived alone, unhappy, or in fear. Now that you are at the end of this book, I invite you to begin your journey, practice the exercises, and embrace the Bounce Back Into You Plan. You can do this! You are the only wonderful version of you there is. The possibilities are endless on how to create the beautiful life you want and deserve.

Just remember that in the end, it's all about self-love and the ability to love others. I waited a very long time to embrace this concept. I hope you will not wait another day. I look forward to hearing from you and about your success.

Epilogue

To this day, I like to call Temple University my happy place. I have been teaching there as an adjunct professor since 2004. My passion is to teach students to believe the following: they can do anything, they ARE smart enough, and they can accomplish whatever they set their sights on. Teaching at Temple allows me to push students to work harder and fine-tune who they are. I am a proud mentor of former students for years. If I can make one student believe in him or herself, I will know that sharing my story was worth it.

It was my positive experience at Temple University that made me want to teach and one day give back to other students what my professors gave to me: a nod and that pat on the back that says, "You are smart enough."

Determined to teach, I went back to school at night to get my master's degree in Elementary Education. There is not one semester that goes by that I don't look a student in the eye and say, "You know you can do this. You know you can work harder and believe in who you are."

One of my proudest moments was in a public speaking class: I was teaching, and a student was standing at the podium. Before every speech, I would say to my students, "Okay, take a deep breath! How does it feel standing up there? You okay?"

And, then this student at the podium turned to me and said, "No, I think I am going to pass out."

There were twenty-two kids in my class. They all turned to me, and I knew it was time to show them their power. I stood up and said, "YES, you can do this!" I walked up to stand next to her. "Look at your classmates," I said. "They are here to cheer you on. This is your safe place to practice your speech. Here is what I am going to do." Then, I asked all the students to take their chairs and turn them around. I shut off the lights, and I said to the student, "Now it's just you and me in the room. I will stand next to you and be here cheering you on. You can do this."

As she started her speech, she was shaking. When she finished, the students turned around and applauded her.

"Okay," I said. "So you did this when their backs were turned, and the lights were out. I would really like it if you would do that one more time, lights off, and the students' heads down." She did it! My final challenge was lights on and the students watching and listening. She did! She was proud of her accomplishment, and so was I. By the end of the semester, she was much more comfortable about her belief that she could give a powerful speech.

I am so blessed to be able to teach. As a young child, I did not think I was smart enough. It is more than possible to bounce back, and change your thinking or ideas. Through lots of self-talk and belief in myself, I now believe that I have what it takes to teach. It's a big responsibility, and I love it. Now I am truly helping others.

The more experience I had as a teacher, the more I realized I wanted to write a book. This book. Originally I decided to write it and share my story, directing the focus primarily toward women. But something wonderful happened: a male student thanked me for influencing him to believe in himself. So now I am proud to say: I am writing this book for all the men and women out there who would benefit from learning the importance of self-love and respect. If we love ourselves enough, no matter what life throws your way, you can always bounce back.

My goal and commitment on a personal and professional level have always been to be a mentor and a role model. As an adjunct professor at Temple University in Philadelphia, Pennsylvania, I have touched the lives of students, young men and women, who need not just a teacher, but a mentor and a role model. Teaching is my passion. My dream is to teach self-love and motivate others to always believe in themselves. And then everything else will fall into place.

My hope is to inspire men and women to believe that alone and all by themselves, they are enough. And to inspire them to smile and remember that in the end, we all have the power to make our dreams come true. I have been looking for romantic love for more than forty years. Take it from me, it can wear you down. But I don't let it. I just keep bouncing back.

Have some fun. I certainly did! Your journey will be an exciting time to really get to know yourself and what makes you "you." I took that journey to be alone and go down a scary road, to look inside myself, and to face my fears and my pain without abandon. What did I really have to lose? Nothing, except a chance to get healthy and know what true, genuine love feels like.

It's a choice. It's always a choice. Never quit on yourself. Make it your choice to succeed, and you will.

Acknowledgments

Gratitude is one of my favorite words. For me it is not just spoken, it comes from my heart. I live my life from a place of gratitude, appreciation and admiration for other people.

I cannot possibly express the amount of genuine gratitude, appreciation and admiration for all the wonderful people who have made an impact on my life and helped me bounce back.

A special *thank you* always goes to my parents for their unconditional love and support. Without my family and all of their love I know I would have made it to where I am today. I am truly blessed with an amazing support team including my aunt Roberta, uncle Ted, cousin Jodi, my brothers Larry and Michael, and wonderful sisters-in-law Laura and Tisa.

We all know I could write a book about my friends and how fortunate I am to have such richness in my life! To all of my friends who have always helped me bounce back, I say, "Thank you for being part of my life, my team and my heart. I treasure all of you."

The last *thank you* goes to Lisa Shiroff, my editor, my publisher and now, someone I call a friend. Lisa is my sunshine. Her influence in my life has been life changing for me. Since the day we met she has kept me on my toes, pushed me, challenged me and, most importantly, makes me better with every phone call, text and email. Together, I know we will continue create books that help people bounce back from life's adversity.

About the Author

Motivational speaker and marketing entrepreneur **Lisa Bien** knows finding success in any area of life requires self confidence and perseverance.

After twenty years of creating successful marketing strategies and public relations campaigns, and in addition to her continuing role as President of B!EN MARKETING GROUP, Lisa is now bringing her trademark energy and passion for storytelling to a more personal level. Lisa regularly serves as a keynote speaker, holds personal development workshops, coaches business professionals, is an author, and hosts her own TV show and YouTube Channel: BounceBackLisaBien.

To learn more about Lisa, about her upcoming appearances, the TV shows, coaching services and to sign up for her newsletter, please visit her Bouncing Back website at:

www.LisaBien.com